W9-ANG-298

From Pulpit to Politics:
Reflections on the Separation of Church and State

WCP

Cleveland, Ohio

Copyright 1999 by Williams Custom Publishing
All rights reserved
No part of this work may be reproduced in any form, or
by any means, without the permission of the publisher.

Published by: *Williams Custom Publishing*, Div.
Lakeshore Communications
24100 Lakeshore Blvd.
Euclid, OH 44123
(216) 731-0234
Visit our home page at: http://www.willese-press.com

From Pulpit to Politics:
Reflections on the Separation of Church and State

Printed in the United States of America

BCDEFG

ISBN 1-893435-01-6

This publication is designed to provide accurate and authoritative
information with regard to the subject matter involved. It is sold
with the understanding that the publisher is not engaged in rendering
legal, accounting or other professional advice. If legal advice or
other expert assistance is required, the services of a qualified professional person should be sought.
- From: **A Declaration of Principles**, jointly adopted by a Committee of the American Bar Association and a Committee of Pub-
lishers and Associations.

Editorial Services and Cover Design: CCS Associates, Hudson, OH
Cover art by Evan Wilcox

FROM PULPIT TO POLITICS

TABLE OF CONTENTS

FROM PULPIT TO POLITICS

FOREWORD

It is with great admiration and respect for the superb intellect, spiritual commitment, Christ-centered calling, and the social and political activism of Dr. Marvin McMickle that I have accepted the invitation to write the Foreword to this necessary book.

As a pastor who has been to jail four times for leading protest demonstrations for social justice, I believe I can speak with some authority after forty years of experience. As a young student, pastor and sit-in leader, I stood alone among my elders in the ministry in 1960. I stood for John F. Kennedy when they voted to endorse Richard Nixon. They voted for Nixon because John F. Kennedy was Catholic. I believed then and I believe now that religious prejudice is as evil as race prejudice.

As one who worked diligently in Jesse Jackson's campaign in 1984, and served as a Jesse Jackson delegate in 1988, and a Bill Clinton delegate in 1996, I believe that participation in the political process is not only a sacred right but a moral responsibility. I believe there

FROM PULPIT TO POLITICS

will always be tension between the priestly and the prophetic. There will always be controversy around the
minister as shepherd of a congregation, and the minister
as a political office holder or candidate for elective office.

Some of the tension and controversy I have referenced will come from peers. Some from the congregation and community, and a significant amount will come
from politicians and elected officials. These powerful
critics seem to say: "Pastor, we want you to give up your
democratic, constitutional, and unalienable right to seek
political office. However, we want you to be 'available'
to help us get elected." Some ministers quietly accept
this type of political-ecclesiastical house-arrest. Some
never have and never will accept such disenfranchise-
ment. Marvin McMickle is a member of the latter group.
He is one who believes in the prophetic and political,
while not demeaning the ceremonial and priestly. If political leadership is a profession too dirty, and an enterprise too wicked for men and women in ministry; then it

FROM PULPIT TO POLITICS

must be too dirty and wicked for our sons and daughters
and sisters and brothers who come to us daily for counsel and advice. Public service is not inherently dirty. It is
inherently dutiful. It calls for men and women of integrity, commitment, and excellence.

Without the prophetic the community has no conscience. Without the political activists who serve with
deep spirituality, social or public policy becomes cruel,
greedy and inhumane, and social justice, truth, love and
reconciliation become the first casualties.

Many politicians want the blessings of the Church,
Synagogue, Mosque and Temple, but do not necessarily
want their creative leadership, thinking and participation. However, we must always make a distinction between "some" and "all". This does not apply to all politicians, just as activism and prophetic leadership does
not apply to all ministers. Paul Tillich defined freedom
as the right to deliberate, decide, and respond. Tillich
also defined sin as estrangement or separation. Separation from God, self, and others. Exclusion and es-

trangement are both sinful and antithetical to the ideals of democracy and the common good. Dr. McMickle provides out of his experience as a political candidate a significant narrative and an interpretive documentation of the pulpit and public affairs.

The pulpit needed prophetic activists to defeat slavery and segregation, colonialism and apartheid, in Africa, Asia, the Americas, the islands of the sea, and everywhere human oppression exists. The pulpit must be an activist pulpit to defeat oppression and injustice. We need a prophetic and politically activist pulpit in order to overcome racism, anti-Semitism, sexism, poverty and violence. We should welcome Dr. McMickle's book, *From Pulpit to Politics*, as an outstanding instrument for dialogue, debate and action, in church, classroom and community.

As these issues and debates continue, it must be born in mind that while elective office is a viable, noble, constitutional, and non-violent means for shaping social, political and/or public policy, it is not the only means.

FROM PULPIT TO POLITICS

The religious right-wing conservatives understand this and are utilizing every resource available to achieve their goals and objectives. They especially employ the new information technology with an almost unprecedented effectiveness. The influence of the religious right-wing conservatives is deep and wide, from local school boards to Congress and the Supreme Court. From presidents to political candidates to federal judges, Cabinet appointments and ambassadorial nominations. From seminary presidents and professors to trustees, textbooks, and curricula. When persons like Marvin McMickle dare challenge and confront these forces, *From Pulpit to Politics*, I believe they deserve our encouragement and appreciation, even if we prefer a different candidate. Dr. Gardner Taylor says we are threatened today with a new tyranny. Each generation must learn and declare — as Thomas Jefferson previously stated — that "resistance to tyrants is obedience to God".

FROM PULPIT TO POLITICS

When Dr. Benjamin E. Mays retired from the presidency of Morehouse College in Atlanta, Georgia, after 27 great years, he ran for public office (the Atlanta Board of Education) and won with grace and excellence. He went on to become the president of that deliberative policymaking body. The first African American to hold that position and Atlanta's first African American Superintendent in public education was appointed under his leadership. Dr. Mays authored nine books and hundreds of scholarly papers during his distinguished career as educator, minister and public servant. He found the time as a young man to travel to India and meet personally with Mahatma Gandhi.

On the other hand, if Dr. Howard Thurman (a former student of Dr. Mays) had chosen elective political office, he probably would not have produced twenty books and plunged the depths of mysticism, while serving as professor, preacher, pastor, Chapel Dean and mentor to thousands. However, he still found the time and courage to join the March on Washington in 1963, with

FROM PULPIT TO POLITICS

Dr. Martin Luther King, Jr., Dr. Mays and those of us who represented a new generation of freedom fighters. He also found the time as a young man to meet personally with Mahatma Gandhi. Every pulpit cries out for a prophetic voice. Every policy-making body cries out for a conscience. Every classroom cries out for truth seekers, and creative teachers for the life of the mind. Every community cries out for love and reconciliation. Marvin McMickle's book points to some of the ways we can respond to the unending cries.

Otis Moss, Jr., D.Min., Pastor
Olivet Institutional Baptist Church
Cleveland, Ohio

FROM PULPIT TO POLITICS

FROM PULPIT TO POLITICS

ACKNOWLEDGMENTS

There are a number of people without whom this book would never have been completed. First and foremost are my wife, Peggy, and my son Aaron, whose love and support over the years have been a constant source of strength and encouragement. I will be forever indebted to my mother, Marthetta McMickle, who sacrificed in ways I will never even know to help me secure my college education. She has always believed in me, even when doing so was little more than "the assurance of things unseen."

I am grateful to Dr. Larry L Macon, Sr., pastor of Mt. Zion Baptist Church of Oakwood Village, Ohio and President of the United Pastors in Mission, for his friendship and support. It was his intervention that directed me to the people who published this book. His scholarly production as both writer and editor is a source of inspiration. I am also grateful to Dr. Otis Moss, Jr., pastor of Olivet Institutional Baptist Church of Cleveland, Ohio. My admiration for him is inestimable, and I

xiii

appreciate his willingness to write the Foreword for this book. He has gone out of his way to encourage me in my ministry since he preached the sermon at my pastoral installation at Antioch Baptist Church of Cleveland in 1987.

There are two men whose presence I felt as I wrote every word of this book, Samuel D. Proctor and Lawrence N. Jones. They presided together at my wedding ceremony and have been both friends and critics for twenty-five years. They encouraged me to do the best with what God has given me, and have never allowed me to settle for anything less than my best. Every young preacher needs such a presence in his/her life. In addition to them, I had another mentor in the person of W. A. Jones, Jr. of Brooklyn, NY. He has had a hand in every phase of my ministry and I love him like a father.

Finally, I want to dedicate this book to black preachers from Hiram Revels to Adam Clayton Powell, Jr., to Floyd Flake — who have dared to cross the lines that have long separated church and state in America, and to make the move *From Pulpit to Politics*. This book is written to celebrate their achievements and their daring. This book is also written in the hope that other preachers, black and white, will follow their example. At the local, state and national levels, there is a role that members of the clergy can play in the political process. The Religious Right is already engaged, but their agenda is far too limited and their ranks are far too narrow to leave me feeling content. Revels, Powell and Flake have led the way. It is past time for others of their profession, with a similar commitment to justice and freedom, to enter the fray and continue the work begun by these trailblazers.

FROM PULPIT TO POLITICS

PREFACE

The credit goes to that man who is actually in the arena, who strives valiantly,
who knows the great enthusiasms and the
great devotions. Who spends his life in a
worthy cause. Who, at best knows the tri-
umph of high achievement. And who, at
worst, if he fails, at least fails while daring greatly. So that his place shall never
be among those weak and timid souls
who know neither victory nor defeat.

Theodore Roosevelt

This book is offered as a challenge to members of
the clergy and any active member of a faith community
to enter the political arena at every level of government
from the local precinct to the United States Congress. It
is also written as a rebuttal to those persons who would
seek to argue that such involvement by the clergy or active lay persons is a violation of the principle of the
separation of church and state. Too many people with
roots in various faith communities, with too much to of-

fer in terms of energy and insight, have sat on the side-lines of the American political system.

They have done this while the nation has suffered from voter apathy, partisan bickering that has resulted in legislative gridlock, and sexual escapades in the White House that have reduced the Presidency to the butt of jokes for late night TV shows. Political campaigns have become extended attack ads where candidates dig up dirt on each other, rarely if ever discussing the pressing issues facing their ward, district, state or the nation as a whole. The cost of campaigns continues to escalate, as does the cost of supporting various government programs and services. We complain about this in our churches, synagogues and mosques, but seldom do we take our interest in these issues to another level of involvement.

This book is a call for people of faith to get involved in politics. And it attempts to set forth in biblical, historical, and constitutional terms, the reasons why such involvement is both necessary and appropriate. Involvement can include speaking about social and political issues in an attempt to influence political officeholders and to shape public opinion within the electorate as people consider how, or for whom, they will vote. Involvement can also include direct support of a candidate for political office who shows particular interest in the issues and causes that resonate within the faith community. In this same vein, it can involve urging persons to run for office, and supporting them in the process, because of the skill, passion, or unique experience they may possess.

Third, and most important for this book, is the possibility that members of the clergy will become directly involved in politics by running for an elective office themselves at any of the levels of government, from Precinct Leader to a member of the United States Congress.

This book is also designed to respond to those, both inside and outside of the faith communities, who argue that such involvement in politics by a member of the clergy is a violation of the idea of *separation of church and state.* I trace the origins of that idea back to Thomas Jefferson in a letter he wrote to a Baptist group in Danbury, Connecticut in 1802. I will show that the phrase, "separation of church and state" is not found in the U.S. Constitution, even though a number of U.S. Supreme Court rulings have tried to interpret what is meant by the phrase in the First Amendment which says, "Congress shall pass no law concerning the establishment of religion or the free exercise thereof."

This book also answers those who suggest that political involvement by a member of the clergy is incompatible with the teachings of Jesus. When Jesus says, "Render unto Caesar the things that are Caesar's, and unto God the things that are God's", is he arguing against political involvement by pastors and preachers, or is he simply urging people to pay their taxes? When he warns that "No man can serve two masters", is he urging members of the clergy to avoid political involvement, or is he warning believers about the love and the allure of money? I will argue that neither biblical nor constitutional principles are violated when a member of the clergy seeks to hold public office at any level of government.

I will show that within the African American community in particular, the oldest, continuous model of political leadership has been the black preacher. The preacher has been the group leader of black people in America since the days of antebellum slavery. The preacher has been serving in political office in America since the Rev. Hiram Revels was elected to the Mississippi State Legislature in 1867 and was appointed to the U.S. Senate from Mississippi in 1869.

I will show that over 100 black preachers served in various political offices during the Reconstruction era alone. Seven black preachers have served in the U.S. Congress in the last thirty years. Presently, black preachers are serving in political offices at various levels of government in communities across the country. Many are serving, and many more are needed to join them in continuing to provide political leadership to the black community, and to the nation.

The Religious Right and the Christian Coalition have not been halted or hindered by concerns about crossing the line between church and state. These groups have placed a virtual stranglehold on one of the major political parties in this country. They are imposing upon the nation a narrow and punitive sense of what constitutes Christian values. Other voices must be heard from within the faith community, beyond the voices of such clergy persons as Jerry Falwell, Pat Robertson and D. James Kennedy. And those voices must be heard *now!* This book is a call to action to preachers and pastors, black and white, to consider broadening the focus of their ministry *From Pulpit to Politics.*

Much of my own passion about this topic grows out of my own campaign for a seat in the U.S. Congress in May of 1998. It was during that campaign that I discovered how many voters there are who still believe that there are scriptural and constitutional prohibitions regarding the involvement of the clergy in the political process. I was not successful in my quest for that position, though I still serve in another elected office on the Shaker Heights Board of Education. However, this book is not about me or that campaign, though that is its point of departure. This book is about what is happening in America at the turn of the 21st century, and who needs to become more engaged, especially at the political level, if our society is to endure, and if justice and righteousness are ever to reign upon the earth.

We have talked about the problems long enough. The credit goes to those persons who are actually in the arena.

The Rev. Marvin A. McMickle, Ph.D.

Cleveland, Ohio

Advent, 1998

FROM PULPIT TO POLITICS

In his book, *Christian Countermoves In A Decadent Culture*, he makes a point that very nearly mirrors the views of Brown. Henry says:

> Does the church belong in politics?....Since God wills the state as an instrumentality for preserving justice and restraining disorder, the church should urge members to engage in political affairs to their utmost competence and ability, to vote faithfully and intelligently, to engage in the public process at all levels, and to seek and hold public office.[2]

The only warning that Henry offers, and one with which I am in full agreement, is that "The church is not to use the mechanisms of government to legally impose upon society at large her theological commitments."[3]

I argue in the pages that follow that all members of the clergy should give consideration to what Brown and Henry have suggested, and to these three ways, among other possibilities, in which their involvement in politics can be approached. Because I viewed politics both as a means of grace, and as a responsible way to act out my faith, I made the decision to run for a major political of-

Chapter One: The 1998 H. R. Race: Into the Arena

"Any Christian worth his salt knows that in this day and age there is an imperative laid upon him to be politically responsible. When one considers the fateful decisions which lie in the hands of the politicians, and the impact which these decisions will have for good or ill upon the destinies of millions of people, it becomes apparent that in terms of trying to implement the will of God, however fragmentarily, politics can be a means of grace. Christians may not retreat behind the specious excuse that "politics is too messy." Politics has become an arena where the most fastidious Christian must act responsibly and decisively if he is not to be derelict in his duties."[1]

Robert McAfee Brown
Christianity and Crisis
January 19, 1953

These words from Robert McAfee Brown serve as the point of departure for this book that seeks to analyze how people whose vocations are primarily defined by

FROM PULPIT TO POLITICS

the work they do in the pulpit can, and should, involve themselves in the political arena in American society. Two phrases in particular, from this statement by Brown, must be given serious consideration. The first is that "politics can be a means of grace." Is it possible that God can work out His will for our lives and for this world through the active involvement of Christian people in the political process?

Can the power invested in those who shape public policy be used to establish a more just and humane society, as those persons who hold that power are informed and influenced by the tenets of their religious faith? How does such an idea as "politics as a means of grace" raise concerns about the principle of the separation of church and state?

The second phrase from Brown that bears further consideration is the notion that "Christians must act responsibly and decisively within the political arena if they are not to be derelict in their duties." Can it be said that active involvement in the political arena is a necessity

FROM PULPIT TO POLITICS

for Christians, because of the power and influence enjoyed by elected officials to touch and impact the lives of so many people, in so many ways? Brown suggests that this is precisely the case, and I wholeheartedly agree with his assessment.

These words from Brown, written almost a half-century ago, came in the context of his involvement in the re-election campaign of Eugene McCarthy as a member of Congress from Minnesota. Brown, an ordained minister, wrote them while he was serving on the faculty of a college affiliated with the Presbyterian Church. However, they raise a series of questions that are equally relevant and compelling today, concerning how members of the clergy should be engaged with the political arena. First, when is it appropriate for members of the clergy to speak about and advocate for specific political issues? Such utterances can come not only in sermons delivered from the pulpit, but also through active involvement in agencies that address various issues. Opinions can also be voiced by writing editorials to local

3

FROM PULPIT TO POLITICS

newspapers that attempt to clarify or shape public opinion about those issues. Second, is it appropriate for members of the clergy to work in the election campaigns of other persons who are running for office, knowing that within their congregations there may be persons who support other candidates for the same office? Finally, what are the pros and cons of members of the clergy running for and serving in elective office themselves? This book seeks to encourage members of the clergy, as well as devoted lay persons, to see opportunities for their political involvement in all three areas.

I do not assume that all clergy agree with Robert McAfee Brown's assessment of the importance of Christians being actively involved in politics. Many in the church community may perceive him as representing a theological perspective that is too liberal for their liking. Such persons might be more influenced by the views of someone within the more conservative ranks of the American evangelical church, such as Carl F.H. Henry, founder and former editor of *Christianity Today*.

FROM PULPIT TO POLITICS

In his book, *Christian Countermoves In A D*̲ ̲.̲.̲.̲/̲.̲.̲
Culture, he makes a point that very nearly mirrors the
views of Brown. Henry says:

> Does the church belong in poli-
> tics?....Since God wills the state as an in-
> strumentality for preserving justice and
> restraining disorder, the church should
> urge members to engage in political af-
> fairs to their utmost competence and
> ability, to vote faithfully and intelligently,
> to engage in the public process at all lev-
> els, and to seek and hold public office.[2]

The only warning that Henry offers, and one with which
I am in full agreement, is that "The church is not to use
the mechanisms of government to legally impose upon
society at large her theological commitments."[3]

I argue in the pages that follow that all members of
the clergy should give consideration to what Brown and
Henry have suggested, and to these three ways, among
other possibilities, in which their involvement in politics
can be approached. Because I viewed politics both as a
means of grace, and as a responsible way to act out my
faith, I made the decision to run for a major political of-

fice in 1998. During my years in the ministry, I have tried to shape public policy, and people's understanding of policy issues, not only through sermons, but also through active involvement in community and civic groups that focused on a wide range of issues. These have included matters ranging from civil rights to prison reform and the re-entry of convicts into society, public education, battered women, support services for AIDS victims and their families, and quality of life issues. My advocacy has extended into an active involvement with the news media in my community, giving interviews on radio and television, and writing occasional editorials in the daily paper. While people have not always agreed with my positions on issues, rarely, if ever, has anyone challenged the appropriateness of a member of the clergy being involved in social issues.

I have been actively involved in supporting the political campaigns of other persons who were seeking election to public office. The Antioch Baptist Church, where I serve as Pastor, has welcomed and introduced any number of candidates to the congregation on a Sunday morning. We have allowed persons to distribute campaign materials both inside and outside the church. We have held special forums so that candidates could speak about their aspirations and receive questions from the public.

On November 1, 1994, President Bill Clinton spoke from the pulpit of this church as he attempted to address issues of urban policy and civil rights, both to the audience gathered in front of him and to the entire nation through the national news media that came with him that night. Other persons running for, or serving in federal level positions have also spoken to the congregation from the pulpit, including Congressmen Louis Stokes and John Lewis, and Senators John Glenn and Howard Metzenbaum.

On several occasions I have endorsed candidates for public office, and in some instances have traveled around to speak at various rallies and political party gatherings on behalf of those candidates. I was especially supportive of the first election campaign of Michael R. White when he sought the office of Mayor of the City of Cleveland. Subsequently, I served in several appointed, voluntary roles within his first administration. I have attempted to be helpful to a number of persons whom I thought could transform political office into a means of grace. This involvement has, at times, been somewhat more controversial than simply sharing my own political views in letters to the editor or in interviews. However, the controversy has more often been in relation to *who* I was supporting, not the fact that I was supporting a candidate for political office.

The Race to Succeed Louis Stokes in the U.S. Congress

General acceptance of my involvement in politics dramatically changed after February 19, 1998. That is the day I filed my petitions with the Cuyahoga County Board of Elections and began my own campaign to be elected to public office. I determined to run for a seat in

FROM PULPIT TO POLITICS

the United States Congress from the 11th District of
Ohio. I was not so much seeking to change professions
from pastoral minister to professional politician as I was
attempting to embody the words of Robert McAfee
Brown and "act responsibly and decisively....not be
derelict in my duty as a Christian...and turn politics into
a means of grace."[4] I was attempting to use political office as Carl F.H. Henry had suggested, as "an instrumentality for preserving justice and restraining disorder."[5]

The congressional district in which I ran includes
most of the east side of the City of Cleveland and many
of the eastern suburbs of Cuyahoga County, in northeast
Ohio. Louis Stokes had represented this district since
1969. The district was created by a United States Supreme Court ruling under the Voting Rights Act. That
ruling created what was then known as the 21st Congressional District, now the 11th district, allowing for the
possibility of an African American to be elected to Congress from Ohio.[6] This remains the only district in Ohio

FROM PULPIT TO POLITICS

from which an African American has been elected to the Congress in the history of the state.

During his tenure in office, Louis Stokes became one of the most respected men in Washington, D.C., and easily the most revered man in Greater Cleveland. However, after thirty years in Congress, Stokes decided not to seek another term in office. Along with four others, I sought election in the Democratic Party primary to be held on May 5, 1998. The ten weeks between the filing deadline of February 19th and the May 5th primary election were among the most exhausting, exhilarating and enlightening times of my life.

I had run for and won political office before, but never at this level. I had twice been elected to the Shaker Heights (Ohio) Board of Education. In fact, I had just begun my second term on that Board when Stokes made the announcement that he would not be running for re-election. I was elected with 6010 votes, a sizeable number in a suburban community like Shaker Heights with 32,000 residents. However, the 11th Congressional Dis-

trict covers twenty-two separate towns,
over 560,000 residents. Running for a pc
is a massive undertaking requiring energy and stamina
on the part of the candidate far beyond that involved in
running within just one town.

The Election Campaign: My Platform

The first task was to create a campaign platform
upon which to run. In a telephone conversation with one
of my supporters, Amy Kaplan, something we called
"The Eight E's" was born. We ran our entire campaign
around eight ideas all beginning with the letter E. They
were *employment, education, economic development,
elderly, environment, equal opportunity, enforcement of
the law* and *enlargement.* The scope of this platform
meant that we were defining our target audience as all
twenty-two towns and cities in the 11th district, and not
just the black population centered in the City of Cleveland.

FROM PULPIT TO POLITICS

For most of the campaign, this was the only political platform put forward. Eventually, other candidates also issued positions, but it was amusing to notice how many of them involved words that began with the letter E, or were our ideas stated in slightly different ways. The distribution of this eight-point platform at the first candidates' debate caused the skeptics and cynics to take my campaign seriously. I am convinced that the platform was the basis for all the endorsements we eventually received.

There were many other tasks that had to be accomplished, and there was very little time in which to do them. Scores of campaign workers had to be organized to staff telephones, stuff thousands of envelopes, contact absentee voters, and work on scheduling the candidate into Ward Clubs and neighborhood forums. We had to plan for and prepare media releases and campaign commercials, distribute printed literature and front lawn signs, and complete a dozen other tasks necessary if the political campaign was going to have a reasonable

FROM PULPIT TO POLITICS

chance of being successful. All of this had to be generated within a matter of a few weeks.

Thank God for Eva Bekes and Sam Tidmore, who worked tirelessly to bring order out of chaos. Through their tireless efforts, an efficient campaign team was assembled, and a first-rate campaign effort was launched. Many members of the team were members of Antioch, others were persons I had worked with while running for office in Shaker Heights or in my clergy association, and the rest were concerned citizens who walked in off the street and volunteered their time and energy. I will never forget the first campaign meeting that was held with just ten people seated in a circle in my living room. By election day our list of active campaign supporters and contributors had swollen to over four hundred and fifty persons. We raised in excess of $85,000, and ran a first-class political campaign. I will forever be indebted to those who gave so much to my campaign.

FROM PULPIT TO POLITICS
Stephanie Tubbs Jones

The challenge of organizing a political campaign was not as difficult for two of my opponents in the Democratic primary. Stephanie Tubbs Jones, the Cuyahoga County Prosecutor, was an eighteen-year veteran of running campaigns and serving in a variety of elective offices. She was the clear front-runner in the race because: she was a formidable campaigner, she had an established political base, and she enjoyed the invaluable magic of name recognition. Within the first few weeks of the campaign, she was endorsed by the Cuyahoga County Democratic Party, the Cleveland AFL-CIO, and dozens of local political office holders throughout the 11th Congressional District. These endorsements assured her of monetary support and an army of campaign workers. They also proved to be an advantage that my own campaign effort was never able to overcome.

My campaign did offer a certain logic as to why I ought to be preferred over Mrs. Tubbs Jones. The position she held as County Prosecutor was far more important to the African American community than becoming a freshman member of Congress in the minority party. She was giving up a job for which she was *uniquely* qualified, in order to pursue a job for which others were equally qualified. We argued that her election would result in a political net loss. The power of her present office, which included not only her own personal involvement but the work of the nearly 150 Assistant Prosecutors who worked under her direct supervision, was immense.

Some of her predecessors in that office had been viewed as using the power of the office to harass and intimidate the black community, especially prominent members of that community. All of the harassment had stopped under Jones. She also had done an outstanding job in hiring and promoting other African American lawyers within her office. While she served, she was the only African American County Prosecutor or District Attorney in the State of Ohio. Regrettably, there was no other African American attorney positioned to be appointed to fill her unexpired term upon her election to the seat in the Congress.

It was clear to me that we in the black community were on the verge of losing a job of immense power in exchange for another job, where power was in direct relation to seniority. The winner of the November election would have no seniority, thus very little power or influence in Washington, D.C. for many years to come. Two jobs in politics are better than one. Losing the position of County Prosecutor in exchange for a seat in the Congress may have been a good career move for Jones, but it remains a great political net loss for the African American community of Greater Cleveland.

While many persons understood my argument, many more were extremely angry with me, believing that I was attempting to impede the natural career progression of Mrs. Jones. Who was I to suggest to her what career moves she should and should not make? She also turned my own argument against me in a very effective way, saying that if she was as effective as I said she was in her present job, *"Just think what a great job I can do for you when I get to Washington!"*

Add to that perceived insult to Mrs. Jones the power of the women's vote whenever a qualified woman is among the candidates, and my argument largely fell on deaf ears. Her political experience, personal popularity, name recognition and proven electability resulted in her being overwhelmingly elected in the primary. It also did not help my cause that the incumbent, Louis Stokes, helped arrange a fund-raiser for her in Washington, D.C. Not only did that event raise money that could be applied to her media campaign, but it also sent a signal to many throughout the 11th Congressional District that Stephanie Tubbs Jones was the preferred candidate of Louis Stokes. That endorsement, or perception of an endorsement, would, on its own, have been enough to guarantee victory to whichever candidate was fortunate enough to receive his blessing.

FROM PULPIT TO POLITICS

One other factor that could not have been anticipated was the link between Jones' campaign and the efforts of Jimmy Dimora, the Mayor of Bedford Heights, and the County Democratic Chairman. Dimora was running in the same primary for the office of County Commissioner. He engaged in a massive get-out-the-vote effort to help him in his election effort. Only 27% of the registered voters turned out for the primary, and those who did were largely party regulars and members of organized labor who had been mobilized to support Dimora. Once they got to the polls, they voted the party line with very few exceptions. All things considered, this was not a race for me to win. It was always a race that Stephanie Tubbs Jones would have to lose, and she did not lose the race.

Efforts quickly got underway to identify and build support for another African American who could fill the position of Cuyahoga County Prosecutor. James Draper, the Cuyahoga County Public Defender, emerged as the only African American candidate for the position. A former police officer, a law enforcement professor, a practicing attorney for over thirty years, and an administrator of a major department within the county criminal justice system, he is clearly the most qualified person seeking the office. However, the Democratic Party Central Committee and all of the ward and precinct leaders vote to fill the position. It will be a political appointment, and whoever does the best job of appealing to those party leaders will fill the unexpired term. The position will be up for an open election in the year 2000. I am pleased to serve as the co-chair of Draper's campaign, and I hope he will be successful in being appointed the next Cuyahoga County Prosecutor. If he is not appointed to the position, I sincerely hope he will run for the job in the year 2000.

Jeffrey Johnson

The other major contender in the race was Jeffrey Johnson, an eight-year member of the Ohio State Senate who had also served for six years as a member of

Cleveland City Council. He, too, had an established political base that he had nurtured over several election campaigns. His campaign suffered a severe blow when he was indicted for seven violations of campaign finance laws. He vehemently insisted that he was innocent, and I went out of my way to publicly support him when those charges were first raised. It seemed clear to me at the time that he was the intended target of the ugly side of the American political system — charging someone with a crime and rendering them guilty until they prove themselves innocent. Several months after the May 5th primary the whole matter vanished from view. This further strengthened the perception that his campaign was sabotaged. The charges, however, continue to plague Senator Johnson. In the Fall of 1998, the charges were presented to a grand jury and the possibility of further legal complications continues.[7]

However, for the Primary election, the damage had been done. The charges greatly impeded his ability to raise money for his campaign. It caused many people to write him off as being "unelectable." It frustrated him at every candidates' debate, because the questions about the indictments would be raised and the cloud of suspicion would once again hang low over his candidacy. Nevertheless, he campaigned fiercely. He ran on the claim that his fourteen years of experience as a legislator at the municipal and state levels made him the most qualified person to be elected to a national legislative position.

As I reminded him throughout the campaign, the job we were all seeking was a seat in the United States House of Representatives, not the United States House of Legislators. My point was that there are many skills and talents, beyond being a member of the State Legislature, that are needed if someone is going to be an earnest and deliberate representative of the many and varied groups that lived in the 11th Congressional District. Part of the problem with our representative form of government in America is that those who currently hold office are not reflective enough of the age, race, gender, income, vocational and ethnic diversity of this country. Possessing a law degree does not necessarily equip a person to be competent in discussing and resolving questions about farm subsidies, defense spending, welfare reform, charter schools and voucher programs, or even the mandatory sentences that ought to be imposed upon those convicted of crimes. Senator Johnson was certainly qualified for the position and would have made an outstanding congressman. However, neither Jones nor myself were willing to concede that not having had any legislative experience was a fatal flaw insofar as our qualifications to serve in the Congress were concerned.

Johnson received strong support from groups of African American men living in Cleveland and East Cleveland. They believed that his base in the urban core of Cleveland made him a stronger candidate than myself, because my base was perceived to be in Shaker Heights and the other, more racially-mixed eastern suburbs. Despite his hard work and good ideas, his message was not heard, largely because of the indictments against him.

FROM PULPIT TO POLITICS

Still, while he finished third among the major contenders, he trailed me by less than 100 votes. Had those indictments not been issued against him, the race might have taken on a very different shape. I do not know if he would have been able to beat Jones, because Jones also appealed to and lived in the same urban core that was the heart of Johnson's strength. It does seem likely, however, that he would have been able to place second in the race.

Campaign Backdrop: The Untold Story.

This campaign came close to never occurring, though the voters in the district never knew it. Some persons in Greater Cleveland's black community held a meeting one Saturday morning before the February 19th filing deadline, a meeting that was intended to identify a consensus candidate for the Democratic primary. Given the strength of the Democratic Party in the county, whoever won that primary would surely win the November election. Thus, the next Congressman would be selected by a group of thirty individuals. Neither the location nor the participants in that meeting were ever publicly disclosed.

These thirty people would interview the three major candidates. In fact, I was initially not even going to be allowed to appear before the group. Those thirty persons would decide which one person they preferred for the job and would endorse that candidate. The other candidates would then withdraw from the race, endorse the consensus candidate, and the race would be over before it actually began. Whatever happened to democracy?

Such a process was employed thirty years earlier when Stokes was first elected to Congress. Then, the process made sense. There were fourteen candidates vying for the nomination of the Democratic Party. The fear was that such a crowded field might split the black vote and allow a non-black person to be elected. This would have been tragic since the seat was created in order to provide a black congressional representative for that district. Thus, the actions taken in 1968 could easily be understood.[8] However, there was not the remotest possibility of that occurring in the 1998 Democratic primary. Thus, the need for this attempt at selecting a consensus candidate was more difficult to comprehend.

Many of those who were in attendance at this meeting later revealed their own discomfort with the process. They were quickly able to see that such an approach to narrowing the field of candidates for the Democratic primary was inconsistent with the principle of democratic government coined so eloquently by Abraham Lincoln in the Gettysburg Address in 1863, *of the people – by the people – for the people.*

While the meeting did take place, it did not result in a consensus candidate being selected. As a result, along with Stephanie Tubbs Jones and Jeffrey Johnson, I was honored to participate in one of the most spirited, hotly contested, and issues-oriented campaigns that anyone in Greater Cleveland could remember. We never allowed the race to degenerate to name-calling or character assassination. In a series of debates held in churches throughout the district, we discussed not only our respective credentials and experience, but also a wide range of issues. They included such things as Social Security, Medicare, NAFTA, the International Monetary Fund, welfare reform, capital punishment, public education and the perceived dangers of vouchers and charter schools, and much more.

The Campaign Results

The most disappointing aspect of this race was not losing, it was the turnout. I received nearly 15,000 votes in my first run for a major political office, and I received the endorsement of *The Cleveland Plain Dealer*, the editor of *Crain's Cleveland Business Weekly*, and the National Sierra Club. I made a respectable showing, by any measure. However, as stated earlier, only 27% of the registered voters in the 11th Congressional District came out to vote in the primary. Here was a spirited campaign that was discussed for weeks on the front page of the city's daily newspaper. It also received weekly coverage

26

in the *Call and Post*, the paper that focuses on events in the black community. Nevertheless, significant numbers of voters did not care enough about the race to come out and vote. This was the first time in almost thirty years that the congressional seat was open. It was a race that received some national attention because of the prominence of Louis Stokes. Despite all of that, the voter turnout was abysmal. This is a problem not only in the 11th Congressional District of Ohio. It is a matter of increasing concern across the country. Our democracy will be in danger if we cannot recapture the broad interest and participation of *"We the people..."* in the nation's electoral process.

Opposition to My Candidacy

As challenging as it was to mount a first-ever political campaign for a federal level position, that was not the greatest challenge of the campaign. Despite encountering resistance and outright opposition from much of the political establishment, that, too, was not the biggest hurdle I had to clear. Even though I was disappointed by the low voter turnout, neither was that my greatest disappointment. The most sobering and surprising outcome of the campaign was the realization of how many people there were, even within my own congregation, and within my own clergy association, who believed that a member of the clergy serving a local church should not run for, and could not be effective in public office. As one of my campaign workers remarked a few days after the election, "people never forgave you for being a minister."

In a feature story about me and my family in the August 30, 1998 *Cleveland Plain Dealer Sunday Magazine*, Jeffrey Johnson, one of my opponents in the primary, seemed to capture that aspect of the public's sentiment when he said, speaking about me:

> To be a good politician, I think he has to deal with the fundamental question of mixing religion and politics....Although intellectually he can deal with the difference, there are still practical conflicts on a day-to-day basis. In the long run, he's

going to have to choose between religion
and politics. I don't think it's a good balance in the long run.[9]

Here is the tension that must be resolved. Do members of the clergy listen to voices like Robert McAfee
Brown, who challenge us to see political involvement as
a means of grace, and who warn us that we shirk our
fundamental duty if we do not at least attempt to wield
some of the power that effects the lives of so many millions of our fellow citizens? Or, do we placidly accept
the view of those like Johnson who suggest, though
without any clear argument to support their view, that
religion and politics do not mix?

Other members of the local clergy in Cleveland took
opposing sides on the question not only of my candidacy, but also of the involvement of preachers in elective political office. On the one side were persons like
Dr. Otis Moss, Jr., pastor of the Olivet Institutional
Baptist Church, who served as my Campaign Chairman,
was a valued advisor, a major donor, and even appeared
in radio and television commercials in support of my

candidacy. On the other side were respected clergy leaders, good friends and colleagues, who thought that the pastor's place was in the pulpit, not amidst the give and take of politics. One such pastor spoke the sentiments of many in the black church community in the April 29 issue of *The Cleveland Plain Dealer* when he said:

> Congregations sometimes are wary about their ministers personally crossing the line from the religious realm to the political. They may want you to stay in the spiritual sphere, to stay with the flock. They may be suspicious about you delving into the world of smoke-filled backrooms.[10]

I was endorsed and enthusiastically supported by members of my own clergy group, United Pastors in Mission, the largest inter-racial and inter-denominational clergy association in Northeast Ohio. Many of them allowed me to address their congregations on Sunday morning, allowing me to put my candidacy in both a political and a biblical perspective. However, when I solicited the support of the other clergy groups in the community, the most I received was their decision to remain neutral and

FROM PULPIT TO POLITICS

endorse no one in the race. On more than one occasion, I found myself echoing the words of Dante's *Inferno*, when he said "the hottest place in hell is reserved for those persons who, in the time of critical choosing cling to neutrality."

Opposition to my candidacy on the grounds of the church/state issue was not limited to my opponents, many in my congregation, or other pastors in the community. Several other political officials also shared with me the voices of opposition they had heard during the campaign. A black councilmen from one of the suburban communities within the 11th district told me some weeks after the primary that he had repeatedly heard people in his community pointing to the separation of church and state issue as a major factor in their decision not to support my candidacy. A black female state legislator said to me directly, following one of the candidate forums, that I should "stay in the pulpit where I belong."

There seemed not to be any awareness of the fact that seven black clergymen have served in the U.S. Con-

31

gress over the last thirty years. I knew this history from having served for four years on the staff of the Abyssinian Baptist Church of New York City. This is the congregation where Adam Clayton Powell, Jr. had served as pastor for thirty-seven years, and spent twenty-two of those years serving in Congress. My professional development took place in a context where the blending of religion and politics was as natural as breathing in and breathing out.

Powell was not the only clergyman to serve in Congress during my lifetime. He was joined by Andrew Young of Georgia, William Gray of Pennsylvania, Floyd Flake of New York and Walter Fauntroy of the District of Columbia. John Lewis of Georgia and J.C. Watts of Oklahoma are also ordained clergymen. In addition to these seven men, Robert Edger of Pennsylvania was an ordained Presbyterian pastor, and Father Robert Drinan of Massachusetts was a Jesuit priest.

During the campaign, I regularly recalled this list of clergy who had successfully blended religion and politics. I even noted that Powell, Gray, Fauntroy and Flake all maintained their pastorates while serving successfully in Congress. However, that perspective either was not widely enough known, or was not broadly enough shared within the 11th Congressional District of Ohio. It was a significant factor in my defeat.

The Separation of Church and State

This leads to another point of tension that needs to be addressed and resolved. Those who opposed my candidacy because I was a member of the clergy and an active pastor did so on the strength of their understanding of the principle of *"separation of church and state."* Many voters in the district were under the impression that those precise words were found either in The Declaration of Independence or The United States Constitution. They believed then, and may still believe today, that my candidacy was unconstitutional. Those who did not get themselves wrongly entangled in political documents got even more wrongly entangled in a handful of biblical verses that they interpreted to mean that the Bible itself explicitly prohibited what I was attempting to do. They either mentioned *"Render unto Caesar that which is Caesar's..."*, or *"You cannot serve God and mammon."* Worse than being unconstitutional, my actions were also viewed by some as being ungodly. My frustration during the campaign was that the voting public, and many in my own congregation, did not understand either the biblical or constitutional issues insofar as the separation of church and state is concerned.

In the face of this, I just kept thinking about the words of Robert McAfee Brown and Carl F.H. Henry. Brown said, *"Any Christian worth his salt..."* He did not say, or in any way imply, that his words were limited to *"Any LAY Christian worth his salt..."* He said simply, *"Any Christian..."* Henry said, *"The church should encourage members..."* He did not suggest that the clergy should be excluded from that charge. And I also kept remembering the nine clergymen who had served in Congress over the last thirty years.

FROM PULPIT TO POLITICS

The challenge I had to face, but could not overcome, was the notion that as a member of the clergy and a pastor of a local congregation, I should not be in the race. That idea, rooted in people's understandings of certain political and biblical principles, was a formidable obstacle. It was far more difficult to respond to than anything else in the campaign, because it did not challenge what I thought or how I might perform in office. It challenged who I was. I needed more than the words of Robert McAfee Brown or Carl F.H. Henry to meet this challenge. Unfortunately, I could not devote the time to this challenge during the short ten weeks of our campaign. However, I have the opportunity to address these questions in this book.

Here is an opportunity to reflect more carefully upon the issue of separation of church and state, to examine the origins of the term, and consider what it was and was not intending to accomplish. Here is also an opportunity to take a look at the historic role of the preacher in the black community, to see if what I was attempting was

35

actually a significant break with my intended role as
shepherd of the flock of God, or was consistent with the
dozens of black clergymen before me who had served
both church and state. Finally, both in sermon and essay
form, here is an opportunity to look at some of the biblical passages that were thrown at me during the campaign, to see if they carry the message that many were
ascribing to them.

This book comes too late to affect my political campaign. However, it may prove to be of some assistance
to some other pastor or clergyperson who, while in the
pursuit of elective office, is confronted with the same
challenges that I encountered. It will also shed some
light on how the issue of separation of church and state
can be more broadly understood by the voting public. I
believe that Robert McAfee Brown was right in 1953
when he saw politics "as a means of grace." I agree,
when he says that Christians are derelict in their duty if
they do not attempt to exercise some influence in that
arena. I believe that Carl F.H. Henry was right in 1986,

when he saw politics "as an instrumentality for preserving justice." I hope others of my vocation will seek to make the move *From Pulpit to Politics.* I offer this book in support of their efforts. Their involvement can help make politics "a means of grace" and "an instrumentality for preserving justice."

Notes: Chapter One

[1]Robert McAfee Brown. "Confessions of a Political Neophyte". Christianity and Crisis 12.24 (1953): 186.
[2]Carl F.H. Henry. Christian Countermoves in a Decadent Culture. (Portland: Multnomah Press, 1986) 118.
[3]Henry 118.
[4]Brown 186.
[5]Henry 118.
[6]Carl B. Stokes. Promises of Power: Then and Now. (Cleveland: Friends of Carl B. Stokes, 1989) 71.
[7]Mark Rollenhagen, "Prosecutors Outline Corruption Case", The Cleveland Plain Dealer, 27 October1998: 1B.
[8]Stokes 71-72.

FROM PULPIT TO POLITICS

[9] Jessie Tinsley. "Saving the Soul of the City", The Cleveland Plain Dealer Sunday Magazine, 30 Aug. 1998: 16.

[10] Joe Hallett. "Candidates seek black ministers' support", The Cleveland Plain Dealer, 29 April 1998: 1A.

Chapter Two: Voices from the Crowd

Regarding the separation of church and state, there were two overarching issues that made my congressional campaign interesting. The first was the simple fact that the 11th Congressional District of Ohio is home to the most diverse group of religious traditions to be found anywhere in the State of Ohio. It is impossible to win an election without interacting with all these groups. It proved to be just as impossible to win and hold the confidence of those various communities of faith. There seemed to be something about my candidacy that made persons in each of those groups uncomfortable. The issue of separation of church and state was how their discomfort was framed, but the precise areas of discomfort varied from one group to the next.

FROM PULPIT TO POLITICS

Demographics of the 11th Congressional District

The Jewish Community

The 11th Congressional District is home to a large and diverse Jewish population. Over the years I have enjoyed a good working relationship with many in the Jewish community. I worked with the Cleveland Jewish Community Federation on a trip to Israel and Senegal that involved 25 area educators in 1992. My own congregation is involved in an on-going partnership with Temple Emanu El in University Heights. I have spoken from the pulpits of three Reform congregations in the Greater Cleveland area, and I was invited to appear before the Cleveland Board of Rabbis to discuss my political platform. Several members of the Jewish community were on my campaign staff, hosted neighborhood fundraising events, and worked in other ways to support my campaign.

However, there was an obvious concern from many within the Jewish community, especially among the

FROM PULPIT TO POLITICS

Conservative and Orthodox groups, with whom I had little or no working relationship. Would I as a Baptist minister use a seat in the U.S. Congress to pursue such sectarian issues as mandatory school prayer, or the restoration of the observance of Christian holidays in schools and other public places? Would the tolerance for religious diversity that has protected religious minorities in America for over two hundred years be disturbed if an active member of the Christian clergy were elected to Congress?

For many in the Jewish community, the idea of an African American minister running for Congress still brings up memories of comments made about Jews by Jesse Jackson in 1984 and Louis Farrakhan in 1988. It reminds others of Rev. Al Sharpton's involvement in the Black-Jewish conflicts that erupted in the Crown Heights section of Brooklyn, New York in the early 1990s. I faced all of these concerns when I ran for the first time for a seat on the Shaker Heights Board of Education. The fact that I won that first election and was re-elected to a second term suggests that the large Jewish community in Shaker was confident that I could function in electoral politics without blurring the lines between church and state. Not surprisingly, Shaker Heights was the only town in the 11th Congressional District that I carried in the May 5th primary. In places where I was less well known, suspicions remained among Jewish voters about my candidacy.

There may have been some uncertainty as to whether I would attempt to align myself with Newt Gingrich and the social agenda in his *Contract With America.* Voters were perhaps concerned that a clergyman in Congress might join forces with groups like the Christian Coalition under Pat Robertson, or the Moral Majority under Jerry Falwell. Many people not schooled in the diversity that exists among Christian clergy on social, doctrinal, and theological issues, may have simply assumed that all Christian ministers support the persons and groups listed above. The fact that I was an active member of the clergy may have caused some to be concerned about the possibility of my using the office to advance the idea of "A Christian America", as is so often spoken of by Christian televangelists who can be heard and seen day and night on various cable television stations.

The concern of the Jewish community is not without merit. Two months after the primary election, I found myself unknowingly involved in an evangelistic effort that did target Jewish families. The Morris Cerrullo Evangelistic Association conducted a weeklong crusade in Cleveland. I was pleased to be part of that effort to bring revival to the Christian community in Cleveland, and make a witness for Christ to all who chose to come. I served as a member of the Executive Committee for that crusade, hosted a pre-crusade prayer rally at Antioch, and even served as a speaker at the School of Ministry during the crusade.

However, I was not aware that the minister from the local Messianic Jewish congregation, sometimes known as "Jews For Jesus", had persuaded the Cerrullo crusade leaders to send a letter to every family in the 44122 zip code region. He proposed this, knowing that the largest concentration of Jewish families in Greater Cleveland was in that region. The idea was to invite Jewish people to an event that was scheduled for the last night of the crusade, and the event was advertised as a service in celebration of the 50th anniversary of the State of Israel.

Cerrullo was himself born into an Orthodox Jewish family and had converted to Christianity. As a result, he has a particular passion for attempting to evangelize others in the Jewish community. In recent years, Cerrullo has gone so far as to mail over one million evangelistic tracts to Jews living in the State of Israel. Written in Hebrew, he was making a case for why they should accept Jesus Christ as the Messiah.[1] As a result of that evangelistic effort toward a targeted Jewish population, a law has been proposed in Israel, and has the support of Prime Minister Benjamin Netanyahu, that would impose a fine and a jail term upon anyone "preaching with the intent of causing another person to change his religion."[2]

FROM PULPIT TO POLITICS

I have no difficulty whatever with Jewish people being challenged by the message of the Gospel. Nor am I opposed to inviting Jewish people to attend an evangelistic crusade. What I opposed was the tactic of cloaking what was the real intent of the letter, which was to evangelize Jews by inviting them to an event that was advertised as being a celebration of the 50th anniversary of the State of Israel. Furthermore, none of us on the Executive Committee knew a decision had been made to send a letter targeted to Jewish families. However, since my name was on the stationary that was used, the calls quickly began coming to me, especially from Jewish voters who had been extremely supportive of my congressional campaign. Calls also came from many Jewish people who implied that it was for fear of this very kind of activity that they opposed my candidacy.

The concerns that were expressed to me dealt first with how the names of Jewish families ended up on a list used by a Christian evangelist. Of even greater concern to the callers was that the event was being planned for a Friday night, when observant Jews would be gathering for their Sabbath services at home and in their synagogues. Furthermore, there was already a major event being planned by local Jewish groups for the 50th anniversary of the State of Israel. They obviously did not want any other event to conflict with, or create any confusion concerning, the gala event they were planning.

It did not take long for me to clarify my position with the Jewish community, or to express to the Morris Cerullo Evangelistic Association my displeasure in not being advised that my name was being attached to what I clearly considered to be false advertising. Spokesmen for Cerullo said that what they were doing was consistent with the Great Commission, to spread the Gospel throughout the world and make disciples of all nations. I certainly adhere to the Great Commission, but in this instance the tactics were quite deceptive. These tactics are precisely the kind that raises tensions among members of the Jewish community — the kind they felt when con-

FROM PULPIT TO POLITICS

fronted with the prospect of my becoming their Congressman.

The Islamic Community

The 11th district is also home to a thriving Islamic
community comprised of persons from such countries as
Israel, Jordan, Lebanon, and several countries in the Per-
sian Gulf region. One of the major points of tension in
Greater Cleveland over the last five years has been the
presence of Arab grocers operating stores in largely
black, inner city neighborhoods. These Arab merchants
have been the target of dozens of robberies and several
shooting deaths at the hands of black youth. The Arab
community has expressed disappointment that the political leadership of Cleveland has not offered them more
protection. The problems have been exacerbated by
charges that food and dairy products sold in those Arab
owned stores were either over-priced or were spoiled or
tainted. In terms of correcting these stereotypes, the
reader should be aware that persons of Arab/Islamic

background are by no means limited to owners of small grocery stores. They are present at the highest levels of the medical, legal, academic and business communities of Greater Cleveland.

In addition to persons from the Middle East who adhere to Orthodox Islam, the 11th Congressional District is also home to a growing number of African Americans who are affiliated with the Nation of Islam. Elijah Muhammad organized this group in the 1930s. Malcolm X popularized it. Today it is headed by Louis Farrakhan. The local Nation of Islam community meets at Muhammad's Mosque #18 on Kinsman Avenue. Others in the African American community are affiliated with yet another Islamic group headed by Elijah Muhammad's son, Wallace. This community meets at Masjid Bilal on Euclid Avenue. Still other African Americans have simply converted to Orthodox Islam, and have no direct connection to either Elijah or Wallace Muhammad.

FROM PULPIT TO POLITICS

None of these groups has had a long history of political involvement. However, at no point in my campaign did any person from either of those groups express any interest in, or support for my campaign. Minister Kevin Muhammad, East Coast Regional Assistant Minister of the Nation of Islam, observed that his group is not philosophically opposed to the idea of supporting a Christian minister for a political office. He said, "We have no problem supporting any candidate, regardless of any particular affiliation...If you are the best person for the job, then we will back you."[3] I regret that this energetic young Muslim minister was not transferred into the Cleveland mosque of the Nation of Islam until the May 5th election had passed. I believe he would have been more involved than were others in the African American Islamic community, and I look forward to his becoming active in future political campaigns.

I had alienated many within the Nation of Islam when I wrote an editorial, printed in *The Cleveland Plain Dealer*, that expressed my non-support for *The*

FROM PULPIT TO POLITICS

Million Man March that was held in October, 1995. I indicated in that editorial, entitled, *"One Million Men Minus One"*, that I would not be attending or encouraging others to attend that march. I saw it as having no continuing social or political agenda beyond the good feelings it would create within those who would gather in Washington, D.C. on that day. Unlike other Civil Rights marches, this one had no clear legislative target. The 1963 March on Washington was held to force a vote on what would become the 1964 Civil Rights Bill. The 1965 march from Selma to Montgomery (Alabama) resulted in the passage of the 1965 Voting Rights Act.[4] Not only did *The Million Man March* lack a legislative focus, the men returned home without any clear, single, political or socio-economic agenda. It proved to be little more than a feel good session. It began with great promise and high hopes, but due to a lack of focus and follow-up, the event echoes a line from Shakespeare; "Much ado about nothing."

FROM PULPIT TO POLITICS

Interestingly, the 1995 *Million Man March* gave rise to the 1997 *Million Woman March* and two 1998 *Million Youth March* gatherings. Hundreds of thousands of dollars have been spent transporting people to these gatherings across the country, and the organizers of those events would be hard-pressed to point to any substantive achievements that came as a result of any of those gatherings. In a *New York Times* article following the *Million Youth March* gatherings in Atlanta, Kevin Sack observed that, "Beyond a call for voter registration, there was no clear agenda for the Atlanta rally."[5] Sadly, the rally held in New York City two days earlier ended in a melee as police and demonstrators clashed in the streets during the closing moments of the speech by march coordinator Khalid Abdul Muhammad. It may be that this unproductive, but expensive, exercise of staging rallies across the country without any clear agenda has come to an end.

However, because the *Million Man March* had been the brain-child of Louis Farrakhan and Benjamin

FROM PULPIT TO POLITICS

Chavis, who would later convert to the Nation of Islam and become Benjamin Muhammad, my non-support for the march was especially irritating to the Nation of Islam community in the Greater Cleveland area. Any number of people told me that they could not support my candidacy because of the position that I took concerning the march. I missed their support, but I would take exactly the same posture today.

Not only were these marches non-productive, but I was especially unwilling to support the *Million Man March* because of the role played by Benjamin Chavis. As a past president of the Cleveland NAACP, I knew only too well how close Chavis had come to destroying the credibility of that historic civil rights agency through his private conduct, and through his misuse of NAACP funds. It seemed to me, that the whole event lacked the proper focus, and was destined to produce no lasting results. I could not, and did not, support that event. I am sure that it cost me some political support when I decided to run for Congress. Such is the complexity of seeking to represent a district as religiously diverse as the 11th Congressional District of Ohio.

White Conservative Christians

The religious diversity of the 11th Congressional District is not limited to the wide array of Jewish and Islamic groups, who not only view each other with suspicion, but who are also marked by considerable diversity within each of their respective groups. Separation of church and state issues also arose from within the white and black Protestant communities. Within the white Protestant community, opposition came primarily from those who thought me too liberal on a variety of social issues with which conservative Christianity is closely identified.

For instance, many of my white, conservative Christian brothers and sisters are solidly Pro-Life. They hold to the view that all human life is sacred. They have concluded that life is sacred in the womb, from the moment of conception. Abortion is, therefore, both a sin against

FROM PULPIT TO POLITICS

God and an act of murder against the unborn fetus. They call both for a constitutional amendment that outlaws abortion and an end to all uses of federal funds to provide medical coverage for women who opt for this procedure.

I hold a different position, one that I refer to as Anti-Abortion/Pro-Choice. By that phrase I mean that as a pastor, I counsel women not to use abortion as another method of birth control. I urge women to consider all of the options available to them, including adoption or marrying the father and raising the child. I discuss the social, medical and biblical implications of having an abortion. However, having offered that advice and counsel, I firmly believe that a woman ought to be left with the right and the personal responsibility to exercise reproductive choice. I do not support a constitutional ban on abortions, and I do not think we should disallow the use of federal funds to provide medical coverage for women who undergo the procedure. It must be observed, however, that I do not support what is known as late-term or partial birth abortions. I hold to this Anti-Abortion/ Pro-Choice position for many reasons, not the least of which are poverty, immaturity, and the prospects of babies being born who are not wanted and who will not be cared for.

There is a clear class division that can be seen in the issue of abortion. Women who can afford to pay a doctor to perform the procedure, without the use of federal funds, have an option not available to other women who lack such financial resources. Those women living in poverty, on fixed incomes, or living on welfare, will be left with few options except having a child they cannot afford or an abortion procedure at a cut-rate clinic under unsafe and unsanitary conditions. These are the very things the U.S. Supreme Court sought to guard against in the landmark case, Rowe v. Wade in 1973.

While I understand the principle of the sacredness of human life that is at the heart of the Pro-Life argument, there are several things about the Pro-Life position that trouble me greatly. The first is that many persons who argue for Constitutional amendments to outlaw abortion also argue for less and less government involvement in the personal affairs of individual citizens. What action is more personal than reproductive choice? Why is it wrong for the government to interfere in some areas of a person's private life, but acceptable for the government to take the lead in the case of abortion? Why are citizens allowed to exercise choices in some areas of their lives, but not in others?

Why should the government be told to stay out of the question of gun control, but be encouraged to establish regulations for abortion? There is no question that hand guns and rifles have become as much a threat to human life as abortion. Where is the logic? Why do they hide behind the Second Amendment reference to "the right to bear arms" while failing to acknowledge that the reference exists in the context of expressing the need for "a well regulated militia"? How strange that many who are the most ardent critics of abortion are among the chief defenders of the right to bear arms. One Saturday morning I would like to invite them to stop standing in front of abortion clinics holding up pictures of aborted fetuses, and come with me to the local funeral parlor where the victims of hand gun violence are being mourned and buried.

It is equally troubling for me that people who adhere to a strict Pro-Life position are not as outspoken about guaranteeing a quality of life for the children they insist must be born into the world. If you hold a Pro-Life position, should you not also support school levies that support public education? Should you not support tax increases that provide the social safety-net services often needed by children living in poverty? If it is morally right to insist that every child be born, is it not also morally right to insist that every child be assured some minimum quality of life as well?

At an even deeper level, how do those who hold a Pro-Life position separate the value of life in the womb from issues such as capital punishment and war? Capital punishment has not been proven to be a deterrent to violent crimes, largely because people know their appeal process can take up to twenty years. Capital punishment can often be avoided not on the basis of guilt or innocence, but on the basis of income and the ability to hire competent legal representation. Finally, capital punishment is far more likely to be imposed upon non- white offenders in America. It is a practice replete with flaws. Yet, those who argue Pro-Life for the unborn are often yelling the loudest for the use of capital punishment. Why is life sacred in the womb, but not to be defended when confronted with the cruelty and inconsistency of capital punishment?

What is to be made of the apparent contradiction that occurred in Texas, when many in the Pro-Life community rallied to gain clemency for Karla Faye Tucker, the woman who was sentenced to die by lethal injection for having committed two murders using a pick-ax as her weapon of choice? I cynically wonder if those who came to her defense, including The Rev. Jerry Falwell, would have been as aggressive in their defense of a double-homicide convict if that white woman had been, instead, a black male who also expressed a sudden and sincere confession of faith in Jesus Christ?

The views of many in the Pro-Life camp are too narrow and disconnected from the larger issues of life in our society to suit me. Doubtless, my views are too liberal and sympathetic to suit many of these people. Regarding the election, if I had been a lay member of a Christian congregation, I suspect that my views on these issues would have been of interest to those in the conservative camp. But when they considered me as a clergy candidate, they were especially distressed.

This became clear at a lunch meeting that was arranged by someone who belonged to my clergy association. He was attempting to help me build a broader base of support among white evangelicals in the 11th Congressional District. By the end of that meeting, it seemed to me that they were going to be supportive of my candidacy both vocally and financially. However, no one brought up the issue of abortion during the meeting. I was talking about my *Eight E's,* and no one there asked the abortion question. When my views on abortion were made known to them after the meeting, those men were never heard from again for the balance of the campaign.

Here is what I was up against in my congressional race. There were two outstanding opponents. However, there was also the broadly held concern about separation of church and state coming from Jewish, Muslim, and white evangelical Christian circles. For many Jewish voters, there was the concern about my aligning myself with the forces of religious intolerance. Among the Black Muslim groups, there was the concern that I was not aggressive enough in support of the separatist/nationalist agenda they preferred. Among white evangelical Christians, I was much too liberal on the social issues that mattered most to them. This was a formidable set of obstacles to overcome in my first campaign for a major political office. And going beyond my campaign, this is a formidable obstacle for *any* religious leader entering politics to overcome.

FROM PULPIT TO POLITICS

African American Clergy

I feel safe in saying, however, that none of that reluctance or opposition was as difficult to understand or accept as the opposition I experienced from within the circle of African American clergy in the 11th Congressional District. Many opposed me because they believed that political office was no place for a pastor of a congregation. They believed that I should be content to remain with my pastoral work, and leave politics to "the politicians." Many in Cleveland opposed me because, after twelve years in the community, I was still viewed as both a newcomer and an outsider. Who was I to contend for the seat held for thirty years by native-born Louis Stokes, elder brother of Cleveland's first black mayor, Carl Stokes? Two of my colleagues were in the difficult position of wanting to support a clergy brother, but they could not. Stephanie Tubbs Jones and Jeffrey Johnson were members of their congregations. There were also members of my congregation who had been long-time political supporters of either Jones or Johnson. The treasurer of Jones' campaign and two of the top campaign staff persons of the Johnson campaign were members of Antioch. I completely understand and applaud that kind of friendship and loyalty. However, the vast majority of black pastors offered no assistance, no encouragement, and no support of any kind to my campaign.

The basis of their opposition was a combination of their understanding of the church/state issue, and their reading of a few Bible verses which seemed to them to suggest that religion and politics do not mix. I attempted to speak at every clergy association to which I was given access. While there were supportive and sympathetic colleagues in each of these groups, the general tone of my reception was hostile. These men seem to be unfamiliar with the historic role played by so many black preachers in the political arena. They seemed unfamiliar with the fact that nine members of the clergy had served in the U.S. Congress over the last thirty years.

FROM PULPIT TO POLITICS

Perhaps the opposition to my candidacy would have diminished somewhat if I had announced my intention to resign from my pastorate and serve full-time in the Congress. Many people may have opposed me because they did not believe that I could do both of those jobs effectively at the same time. I was certain that it could be done for several reasons.

First, I had served at Abyssinian Baptist Church of New York City, where Adam Clayton Powell was a pastor/congressman for twenty-two years. I knew the staffing, scheduling, and time management issues that had to be employed to do these two jobs. I also knew those black pastors who had served in the Congress while continuing their work in the local church. They included William Gray of Bright Hope Baptist Church of Philadelphia, PA; Floyd Flake of Allen Temple AME Church of Queens, NY; and Walter Fauntroy of New Shiloh Baptist Church of Washington, D.C. Each of these men served in the Congress with great effectiveness while continuing to serve as pastors of local congregations. Before I began my campaign, I met with Louis Stokes to share with him my intentions. We discussed the men I just named, all of whom served with him during his thirty years in the Congress. He knew that this combination of tasks could be done, because he had seen it done. It was for these reasons that I made it clear that I would not resign from Antioch if I were elected to Congress.

There was something else that gave me the assurance that I could handle both jobs. For most of the twelve years I had been at Antioch, I maintained a schedule that kept me travelling throughout the state and across the country. Whether teaching, preaching, or serving on various boards and committees, I was already spending large amounts of time away from the confines of Antioch. My time and energy were being spent finishing a Ph.D.; teaching at Ashland Seminary, Case Western Reserve University, and Cleveland State University; serving on a dozen local boards and agencies; serving as President of the Shaker Heights Board of Education; and for four years serving as the president of the Cleveland NAACP.

From the beginning of my pastorate at Antioch, it was clear to me that the pastor of that church was not expected to sit in the church study and wait for the phone to ring. Since 1928 when Wade Hampton McKinney arrived in Cleveland, pastors at Antioch engaged in wide- ranging ministries throughout the city and across the country. I saw my run for Congress as a natural continuation of a seventy-year style of pastoral leadership.

I reminded the voters that Congress only meets one hundred days each year, and that an effective Congressman is back in the district most weekends. Not only had I met with Stokes to share my intentions, but I also met with Eric Fingerhut to get his reaction to my plan. Fingerhut had served one term in Congress, and knew that the pressures on a first-term member of Congress were very different from those felt by a person like Stokes who was in his fifteenth term. Fingerhut mentioned to me that during his tenure in Congress he would return to the district once, and sometimes twice every week. That conversation helped me to say with assurance that I could serve with effectiveness as a pastor and a Congressman. It was possible to hire persons at Antioch to run the church during the week, retain most of the responsibilities as preaching minister and Senior Pastor, and still be responsive to constituent services. Such technologies as e-mail, faxing, paging, teleconferencing, and the convenience of air travel all worked to my advantage.

Most importantly, given the scandal-ridden nature of Washington, D.C. these days, my campaign workers and I all believed that a member of Congress with a church base would be a breath of fresh air. This was my opportunity to embody the words of Robert McAfee Brown and turn politics into a means of grace. While serving in the political atmosphere of the U.S. Congress, my attachment to a local church would keep me tied to the community, and rooted in the value system I held most dear. In short, I would never have consented to resign from the pastorate in order to enter politics full- time. Such a move would have cut me off from the soil that nurtures my soul. I have never forgotten an admonition given me by my friend and mentor, Gardner Taylor, pastor emeritus of the Concord Baptist Church of Brooklyn, New York. He once told me, *"Cut flowers may look good, but they do not last very long."* I did not want to go to Washington, D.C. as a cut flower.

I did not see running for Congress as a career shift. I saw it as a ministry opportunity. It is for that reason that I hope that many other members of the clergy will seek to serve in all levels of political office. By ministry I do not mean to suggest anything particularly pastoral or sectarian. Instead, I mean addressing issues of justice, equal opportunity, and helping to meet the needs of those the Bible calls *"the least of these"* (Matthew 25: 31-46), which includes the impoverished, the infirmed and the imprisoned. I mean what Amos intended when he said: *"I hate, I despise your feast days, and I will not*

FROM PULPIT TO POLITICS

smell in your solemn assemblies...take away from me the noise of your songs...but let justice roll down like waters, and righteousness as a mighty stream" (Amos 5: 21-24). I mean what Isaiah 58 suggests. Not the practice of religious ritual, or the observance of religious holidays, but *"to loose the bands of wickedness, to deal bread to the hungry, to care for the poor, to cover the naked, and to let the oppressed go free."* I am more convinced then ever that politics can be utilized to serve these ends, and that members of the clergy can play a decisive role in bringing this about. Not to do so, is "to be derelict in our duties."

The Relationship between Religion and Politics

I mentioned earlier that there were two things that made my campaign interesting from a church/state perspective. The first was the religious diversity of the 11th Congressional District. The second thing that made my congressional race so exciting was that it literally coincided with a national discussion about the appropriate relationship between religion and politics. The Council on Civil Society, a panel jointly sponsored by The Institute for American Values and the University of Chicago Divinity School, highlights this ambiguity about the role of religion and religious leaders in contemporary American society. In their document entitled *"A Call to Civil Society"*, the panel points out that in the nineteenth century, as discussed by de Tocqueville, religion was first among America's political institutions because it provided restraining influences that helped individuals sacrifice for the sake of the common good.[6] As a result of several court rulings, suggests the panel, religion has been pushed out of the public sphere. As a result of that, we see an "increased tolerance for self-centered and selfish behavior in all spheres of life."[7] Is the key to restoring America to a civil society a matter of returning religion to the public sphere where it was in the nineteenth century? Or have the repeated attempts to impose religious values upon the broader American society, often through the manipulation of the political process, actually been the single greatest contributor to the loss of civility in our nation?

The most recent attempt to restore religious practices to the public sphere came in the form of the *Religious Freedom Act,* sponsored by Representative Ernest Istook, a Republican from Oklahoma. That bill proposed a constitutional amendment that would allow for prayer in public schools, displays of religious symbols on government property, and the use of tax dollars to pay tuition for students enrolled in religious schools. While the bill did not pass in the Congress, it nevertheless contributed to the debate about the separation issue, and opened the door to more divisiveness both within the religious community itself, and between certain religious groups and the rest of society that may feel that once again religious values and symbols are being imposed upon them.

Some people might assume that a Christian clergyman serving in the Congress would support such a measure as *The Religious Freedom Act.* What the public needs to consider is that some clergy would choose to oppose such a measure, because they understand what a threat such an approach would be to the appropriate boundaries between church and state. There are some clergy persons who would not seek elective office only to advance narrow, sectarian issues. They would support the assertion of Carl F.H. Henry, that "The church is not, however, to use the mechanisms of government to legally impose upon society at large her theological commitments.[8] There are some clergy whose social agenda is neither limited to, or defined by the issues of school prayer, abortion, vouchers for private and parochial schools, or religious symbols in public places.

These clergy, instead, are committed to a just society, to the eradication of drugs, to a government that aggressively attacks the problems of poverty, and to equity in the workplace. Some clergy are more interested in guaranteeing women access to the job of their choice at a fair and equitable wage than they are in denying women reproductive choice. There are some clergy who understand that school prayer, unsupported by adequate school funding, especially in inner city districts, will not fix most of what is wrong in our nation's schools. And there are some clergy who understand that placing religious symbols on the wall of a courthouse is a poor substitute for what the prophet Jeremiah calls for, which is *"To write them on your heart"* (Jeremiah 31:33).

The fact is that clergy in America can belong to the same faith tradition, and even read out of the same Bible, and yet hold entirely different views of what constitutes authentic Christian faith and practice. Peter Gomes points this out in his book, *The Good Book.* In speaking about Patrick Buchanan the conservative columnist, and Jesse Jackson the liberal social activist, he makes this observation:

> Jesse Jackson and Patrick Buchanan would appear to have very little in common except for a delight in addressing audiences. Their visions for America could not be farther apart, and yet both appeal to the vision of the Bible to sustain their own vision, and both regard the Bible as the moral platform upon which

the well being of the republic ought to be
reconstructed. Buchanan argues that we
once had the biblical basis for a civil society and have since lost it; and his goal
is to revive a lost ideal. Jackson agrees
that biblical ideals make for the best of
civil society, arguing that we have not
achieved those ideals, however, and that
change, not revival, ought to be the order
of the day.[9]

Both Jackson and Buchanan have run for President of
the United States, making strong appeals for their sense
of the place of religion in American society. Many
clergy in America resonate with Buchanan's concerns
about "the secular establishment, with its values-neutral
morality, its distrust of religion as fundamentally divi-
sive, and in consequence, its segregation of religion into
the private sphere."[10] While Buchanan is not a member
of the clergy, I agree with the assessment of Gomes:

His message managed to do what a generation of revivalist preachers and evan-
gelists could not do. It has fired up
Christian America and sent it marching
into the voting booths of the nation. First
the Moral Majority and now the Christian

Coalition, command the allegiance of
millions of frustrated American Christians who feel that not only their religion,
but the country which their religion built
and sustained, have been taken away
from them.[11]

While much that Buchanan says resonates with truth, it
is what he and those in the Christian Coalition are not
yet willing to say that drives me, and others like me, into
a different camp of biblical interpretation. For me, the
great frustration is not what America once was, but is no
longer. For me, the issue is best stated by the black poet,
Langston Hughes, who observed, *"O yes, I say it plain,
America has never been America to me. And yet I swear
this oath – America will be. "*[12] And the America I am
anxious to see is not best achieved by the introduction of
such measures as *The Religious Freedom Act.* Instead, it
will be achieved by continued enforcement of the 1964
Civil Rights Bill, the 1965 *Voting Rights Act,* and other
laws already on the books that guarantee the constitutional rights of all Americans.

FROM PULPIT TO POLITICS

I fully understand that not all white clergy agree with the views of Patrick Buchanan and not all black clergy agree with me. In his book, *Dissent of the Governed*, Stephen Carter notes that black Christians tend to be, "on nearly every moral issue, well to the right of the American political mean." He comments on two black women he encountered who "moved from involvement in liberal politics to involvement in conservative Christian groups for no other reason than their perception that, among their natural political allies, their desire to talk about their faith — evangelical Christianity — made them an object of sport."[13]

Thus, I am sure that my views on those social issues not only led to a loss of support among conservative white evangelicals, but among conservative Christians both white and black. However, my intention in running was to advance an alternative vision from that of conservative Christianity, a vision of where faith and public policy ought to intersect. Given the influence of such groups as The Christian Coalition and others, it seemed beneficial for someone with legitimate theological credentials to enter this debate about church and state or religion and politics, so that an authentic debate could occur. It is a great concern to me that the voice of conservative Christianity, defined by such spokespersons as Pat Robertson, James Dobson, D. James Kennedy and Jerry Falwell, is the only one presently being heard on the question of how religion and politics should intersect, and it is sounding forth loud and clear. Albert R. Hunt discusses the growing influence of what he calls "The Religious Right", which includes persons such as Dobson, Ralph Reed, and others. In an article in *The Wall Street Journal*, Hunt argues that "the Religious Right is about politics, not faith."[14] I cannot remain silent and give the impression that those voices speak for me.

The National and International Context

It seems safe to conclude that the issue of separation of church and state will occupy a large place in public debate for many years to come. It will concern us as long as groups like the Southern Baptist Convention call for a boycott of the Walt Disney Company, because it objects to certain of Disney's personnel policies, or the ways in which certain of its cartoon characters are presented on screen. It will be raised when the Wisconsin Supreme Court rules that public funds can be used to support private and parochial schools in Milwaukee. Whether or not a member of the clergy is running for elective office, separation of church and state stands at the center of discussion in American society at the end of the twentieth century.

Many members of the clergy raise the specter of violating this separation principle simply by the way they go about doing their priestly/pastoral ministries. A noteworthy example of this came in New York City, when John Cardinal O'Connor condemned a Domestic Partners Bill pending in the New York City Council. This bill, which would recognize that same sex couples have the same legal standing, and should be allowed to share in all the benefits society offers traditional couples, was assailed by the Cardinal in his Sunday morning homily from the pulpit of St. Patrick's Cathedral. Rudolph Guiliani, the Mayor of New York City, observed, "You know we have a division of church and state in the United States, and it's a healthy one. We're all here because people left other places because someone wanted to enforce their religious viewpoint as the view of the state."[15]

In this exchange between a religious and a political leader there is a clear disagreement over the boundaries that separate church and state in America. Was the Cardinal wrong for using his pulpit to address matters that are essentially political and that were at that moment being debated in a duly elected political assembly? Many who were present on that Sunday disagreed with the Cardinal's decision to address that topic from the pulpit.[16] Was the Mayor wrong in suggesting that the remarks by the Cardinal crossed the line between the separation of church and state? This question is not so easily resolved if you are trying to honor the offices, the views, and the free speech rights enjoyed by an elected official and a church leader in the nation's largest city.

More recently, seven of the eight U.S. Cardinals participated in shaping a statement on abortion that raises some interesting church/state issues. In a document entitled, "Living the Gospel of Life: A Challenge to American Catholics", the Cardinals say, "Catholic politicians are endangering their eternal salvation by supporting laws permitting abortion.[17] They further state that "all Americans, and Catholics in particular, should consider their vote as a creative act of participation in building the culture of life.[18]

Americans may have had questions about separation of church and state raised when they watched the progress of a referendum in Northern Ireland in June, 1998, that would result in a peace accord between Protestants who were loyal to the British government and Catholics who wanted independence. Leading the opposition to the peace accords and vociferously urging all Protestants to vote no was The Rev. Ian Paisley. As both a clergyman and a member of the British Parliament, he has long been a political activist in Irish/ British and Catholic/Protestant affairs. Paisley has never used his position to advance a sectarian agenda. Instead, he has pursued a strict political agenda of "loyalism", urging his countrymen to maintain their ties to Great Britain. Do Americans look at a figure like Paisley with suspicion, fearing that he is attempting to serve two masters? Is that what they fear would happen in this country; that a clergy/politician might use his status within the church community to unfairly influence how others in the faith community should vote on any given issue?

Sermons and the Shaping of Public Policy

In a May 29, 1998 notice on the Internet, a reporter with *USA Today* announced that she was looking for someone who could help her in writing a story about "the future of the Sunday sermon." She wanted to examine the question of whether or not it will ever make a

FROM PULPIT TO POLITICS

comeback as a "locus for social policy."[19] Perhaps she was recalling those years when excerpts from sermons preached in several of the major pulpits in America would be printed the next morning in *The New York Times* and *The Washington Post*.[20] Perhaps she was just recalling how many sermons have been preached that have significantly impacted social policy in America.

Dewitt Holland, in *Sermons and American History* (1971), discusses the many preachers and the sermons they preached that addressed such issues as slavery, secession, war and peace, immigration policies, and the responsibilities of society to its neediest citizens.[21] The reporter's comments reminded me of a sermon by Harry Emerson Fosdick, preached at Riverside Church in New York City in 1933, entitled, *"To The Unknown Soldier"*.[22] In this sermon, Fosdick acknowledges that he was an avid supporter of World War I, believing it to be the war that would make the world safe for democracy. However, the brutality of that war, and the unimaginable death toll that resulted led him to the convic-

FROM PULPIT TO POLITICS

tion that war was no longer an acceptable method for resolving conflicts between nations. Was it a violation of
the separation of church and state for a local pastor,
standing in his pulpit, to encourage his congregation to
"study war no more?"

While Fosdick was preaching against war in New
York City, Peter Marshall was serving as chaplain to the
United States Senate. Between 1947-1949, he was daily
praying for the men who were making decisions about
the shape of the post-World War II world. Their decisions shaped the world for the next fifty years. Marshall
did that while serving as pastor of New York Avenue
Presbyterian Church of Washington, D.C.[23] Were either,
or both, of these preachers violating the principle of the
separation of church and state? Where, exactly, should
that line be drawn, and to what authority do we all look
with equal confidence to make that determination?

On April 4, 1967, Martin Luther King, Jr. also used
the pulpit of the Riverside Church to make his first public statement in opposition to the war in Vietnam, *"A

Time to Break Silence. " He contended that what he was doing was logical and consistent with his role as a Christian clergyman and as a winner of the Nobel Peace Prize.[24] It could be argued that it was his opposition to the war, together with his leadership role in the anti-war movement that swept the country in 1967, that led to his assassination. His speech at Riverside Church was delivered on April 4, 1967. He was assassinated on April 4, 1968. Of course, that could just be a coincidence. Nevertheless, here was another preacher willing to use the sermon as a tool for shaping public policy and national sentiment.

Secular Voices Address the Link between Religion and Politics

The current debate about the separation of church and state is not limited to the voices of clergy. It reaches into multiple areas of American public life. In a recent column, Michael Novak, a theologian at The American Enterprise Institute, notes that calls for a return to viewing religion as an important part of a civil society are also being raised by people not at all associated with any religious community or ideology. He gives special mention to the American author, Norman Mailer, and the President of the Czech Republic, Vaclav Havel. Here are two leading figures from the areas of literature and international politics, both calling for the restoration of religious values in society. Novak may be right when he observes, "When Norman Mailer and Vaclav Havel, ripe with years and not particularly known as pious men, join in emphasizing the new importance of religion, you may be sure that the 21st century will be the most religious in 500 years".[25] Even if no particular religious tradition takes root in the 21st century, talk about the relationship between religion and society, and between church and state will continue to be heard.

U.S. Senator John Ashcroft, a Republican from Missouri, is sponsoring a "charitable choice" provision in pending welfare reform legislation. That would allow churches and faith-based groups that provide a variety of social services to receive federal funds and tax exemption. The son and grandson of Pentecostal preachers, Ashcroft is closely allied with Pat Robertson and the Christian Coalition, and is a strong contender for the Republican Party presidential nomination in the year 2000. His provision is already coming under attack on grounds that it violates the principle of separation of church and state.[26] Thus, the stage already seems to be set for the issues and the people who will keep this issue alive.

Is this simply an instance of what Robert Bellah once defined as America's "civil religion?"[27] Is this push by conservative Christians nothing more than the long- accepted practice that Frederick Gedicks calls, "the utterance of faintly Protestant platitudes which reaffirm the religious base of American culture despite being largely void of theological significance?"[28] Is this push to return God to the classrooms and to the American public square, little more than bowing in the direction of divinity, as when the words, "In God We Trust" are inscribed on the one thing most Americans are inclined to trust, our currency? I think not.

Defining the Issues Where Religion and Politics Intersect

There is a renewed attempt, at least within portions of the Christian community in America, to re-assert the influence of religious values on the shaping of public policy. The question is, which public policies, and shaped in what ways? For some, it is a matter of school prayer, the public display of religious symbols such as the Ten Commandments in a court room, or a crèche on public property. It is constitutional amendments that either protect certain rights or outlaw certain acts.

For others, and I place myself in that group, the struggle is over other issues such as social justice, equal opportunity for all despite race or gender, the care and preservation of the earth, and the hopes of the prophet Micah, that people will "study war no more" (Micah 4:3). It is about eliminating poverty, waging a real war on drugs, ending illiteracy among adults, and confronting the threat of AIDS with a serious financial commitment to prevention and treatment.

The concerns raised in this chapter may have influenced some people as they thought about the prospect of electing an active member of the clergy to the U.S. Congress. However, despite the fact that I was not elected, one fact seems clear: persons motivated by their religious values will continue to press their claims upon society in what Richard Neuhaus has called "the public square."[29] As a result, our nation will be grappling with what the Founders of this republic intended by the concept of the separation of church and state.

Notes: Chapter Two

[1]Gary Thomas. "The Return of the Jewish Church", Christianity Today, 7 Sept. 1998: 66.
    [2]Thomas 66.
    [3]Jessie Tinsley. "Saving the Soul of the City", The Cleveland Plain Dealer Sunday Magazine, 30 Aug. 1998: 16.

[4]Marvin A. McMickle. "A Million men minus one", The Cleveland Plain Dealer, 13 Oct. 1995: editorial page.

[5]Kevin Sack. "Atlanta Rally Unburdened by Ills of Harlem's", The New York Times@aol.com,: 8 Sept. 1998: 1.

[6]David Briggs. "Civil-society panel addresses moral decline and malaise", The Cleveland Plain Dealer, 28 May 1998: 7A.

[7]Briggs 7A.

[8]Carl F.H. Henry. Christian Countermoves in a Decadent Culture. (Portland: Multnomah Press, 1986) 118.

[9]Peter Gomes. The Good Book. (New York: Avon Books, 1996) 53.

[10]Gomes 57.

[11]Gomes 57.

[12]Langston Hughes. "Let America Be America Again", Hope and History by Vincent Harding. (Maryknoll, NY: Orbis Books, 1990) 184.

[13]Stephen L. Carter. The Dissent of the Governed: A Meditation On Law, Religion and Loyalty. (Cambridge, MA: Harvard, 1998) 9.

[14]Albert R. Hunt, "The Religious Right Is About Politics, Not Faith", The Wall Street Journal, 20 Aug. 1998, A15.

[15]Mike Allen. "Cardinal Sees Marriage Harm in Partners Bill", The New York Times, 25 May 1998, 1A.

[16]Allen 1A.

FROM PULPIT TO POLITICS

[17]David Briggs. "U.S. Catholics Urged to Take Abortion Issue to Ballot Box", The Cleveland Plain Dealer, 29 October, 1998: 1A.

[18]Briggs 16A.

[19]Reported to me in a conversation with Dr. Fred Finks, President of Ashland Theological Seminary, Ashland, OH.

[20]Clyde Fant, Jr. and William Pinson, Jr. 20 Centuries of Great Preaching, Volume 12 (Waco, TX: Word Books, 1971).

[21]Dewitte Holland, ed. Sermons in American History. (Nashville: Abingdon Press, 1971).

[22]Paul H. Sherry. The Riverside Preachers. (New York: Pilgrim Press, 1978) 49-58.

[23]Fant et al 5.

[24]James M. Washington. Testament of Hope. (New York: Harper and Row, 1989) 231-244.

[25]Michael Novak. "Answering the big questions", The Cleveland Plain Dealer. 2 June 1998: 9B.

[26]Howard Fineman. "The Gospel of St. John", Newsweek, 1 June 1998, 29.

[27]Robert N. Bellah. The Broken Covenant. (New York: Seabury Press, 1975).

[28]Frederick M. Gedicks. "The Religious, the Secular and the Anti-thetical", Capital U. Law Review 20, (1991): 159, 186.

[29]Richard Neuhaus. The Naked Public Square: Religion and Democracy in America. (Grand Rapids, MI: Eerdman, 1984).

FROM PULPIT TO POLITICS

Chapter Three: It Is Our Right

I need to point out that the actual phrase "separation of church and state" appears nowhere in the United States Constitution. What the First Amendment of the U.S. Constitution actually says, insofar as the issue of religious liberty is concerned, is: "Congress shall make no law respecting an establishment of religion, or prohibiting the free exercise thereof..." There is nothing in this statement, either implicit or explicit, that in any way suggests that a member of the clergy should not serve in elective office.

Origins of the Principle of Separation of Church and State

Ideas about the separation of church and state do not, in fact, have their roots in the U.S. Constitution. Instead, one can trace this notion to the writings of Thomas Jefferson. In an 1802 letter to the Danbury Baptists, Jefferson writes:

FROM PULPIT TO POLITICS

> Believing that religion is a matter that lies
> solely between Man and his God that he
> owes account to none other for his faith
> or his worship, that the legislative powers
> of government reach actions only, and not
> opinions, I contemplate with sovereign
> reverence that act of the whole American
> people which declared that their Legisla-
> ture should "make no law respecting an
> establishment of religion, or prohibiting
> the free exercise thereof", thus building *a*
> *wall of separation between Church and*
> *State.*[1]

This language from Jefferson was incorporated into
two United States Supreme Court rulings. In *Reynolds v.
United States (1878)*, the court said: "In the words of
Jefferson, the clause against establishment of religion by
law was intended to erect a wall of separation between
church and state."[2] This case centered on the practice of
polygamy among Mormons in the nineteenth century.
George Reynolds, a Mormon leader and a practitioner of
polygamy, appealed to the court to be allowed to continue that practice on the grounds of separation of church
and state. Interestingly enough, however, the state did

FROM PULPIT TO POLITICS

breach that wall in this case and upheld the ban on polygamy, thus denying the Mormons protection to practice that aspect of their religious tradition. It seems from
this case, that the separation of church and state was not
an absolute principle.

The issue of separation was further emphasized in
Everson v. Board of Education (1947), in which Hugo
Black, writing for the majority said, "The First Amendment has erected a wall between church and state. That
wall must be kept high and impregnable. We could not
approve the slightest breach."[3] The actual words of Jefferson and the two U.S. Supreme Court rulings that reference his words deal with the coercive power of government either to set up or grant favors to a specific religious group; or to somehow require people to adopt
certain religious views or support through taxation those
institutions that promulgate those views. However, they
do not, in any way, suggest that the election of a member
of the clergy to a political office is an inherent violation
of the principle of separation of church and state.

FROM PULPIT TO POLITICS

More importantly, Jefferson stated something in the
1789 *Virginia Statute for Religious Freedom* that, in my
view, guarantees the right of a member of the clergy to
hold elective office. He said:

> Knowing that our civil rights have no de-
> pendence on our religious opinions, more
> than our opinions in physics or geometry.
> Proscribing any citizen as unworthy the
> public confidence by laying upon him an
> incapacity of being called to offices of
> trust and emolument, unless he profess or
> renounce this or that religious opinion, is
> depriving him injuriously of those privi-
> leges and advantages to which, in com-
> mon with his fellow citizens, he has a
> natural right.[4]

Is it not "injurious of the privileges" of a member of the
clergy to be denied the opportunity to serve in a position
of "public confidence" simply because he is a member of
the clergy, with no evidence to suggest that he would use
that elective position to advance a sectarian agenda?

The diligence and integrity with which The Rev.
John Witherspoon of New Jersey served alongside of
Jefferson in the Continental Congress may have set aside

any concerns that Jefferson, or any of the other founders, may have had about members of the clergy serving in political office. Witherspoon was a Presbyterian clergymen who went on to become the President of Princeton University and the first moderator of the Presbyterian Church in America. He was one of the signers of the Declaration of Independence. There is no record that any member of the Continental Congress objected to the presence of Rev. Witherspoon on the grounds of his being a member of the clergy.

In the 1947 *Everson v. Board of Education* case, the Supreme Court upheld a New Jersey law that required public school districts to transport to parochial schools any students living in that district who opted for those schools. The Court said that the issue was primarily one of safety for students travelling to parochial schools, and not one of providing any direct financial benefit to those parochial schools. Writing for the majority, Hugo Black writes:

> The establishment of religion clause of
> the First Amendment means at least this:

FROM PULPIT TO POLITICS

> Neither a state nor the Federal Govern-
> ment can set up a church. Neither can
> pass laws which aid one religion, aid all
> religions, or prefer one religion over an-
> other.... No person can be punished for
> entertaining or professing religious be-
> liefs or disbeliefs.[5]

Once again, there is nothing that in any way prohibits —
or even warns against — the possibility of a member of
the clergy serving in elective office. More importantly,
why would it not be considered a *punishment* for a person to be denied the right to serve in public office simply
because he is an ordained clergyman, especially if he
campaigns on issues and concerns unrelated to any religious or sectarian concerns?

If the answer lies in the public fear about what that
member of the clergy might do once elected, is that not
denying him/her the presumption of innocence until
proven guilty? Worse still, if the answer is in relation to
what some other member of the clergy has done in terms
of abusing the office, is that not being declared guilty by
an association no more substantial than sharing the same

profession? The record of performance concerning clergy who have served in elective office is available, and is compelling. These legislators have not been the ones behind any legislative actions that generated concerns about the separation of church and state.

The Establishment Clause and Article VI of the United States Constitution

Moving beyond issues of the First Amendment, what are the implications of denying a member of the clergy the right to serve in elective office, in light of Article VI of the U.S. Constitution? This article deals precisely with the issue of whether or not any consideration should be given to a person's religious views as a determining factor in their election to any public office. The article says in part, "No religious test shall ever be required as a qualification to any office or public trust under the United States."

The U.S. Supreme Court has, in fact, made it quite clear that the real issue is not who serves in the govern-

ment, insofar as vocation or religious views are concerned, but what *actions* that government does and does
not take that may favor one religious group or viewpoint
over another. In *Lemon v. Kurtzman (1971)*, the U.S.
Supreme Court established a three-part test to determine
if a governmental action is neutral toward religion. The
court ruled:

> First, government institutions or legisla-
> tion must have a secular purpose; second,
> the primary effect must be one that nei-
> ther inhibits nor advances religion. Third,
> there must not be an excessive govern-
> ment entanglement with religion.[6]

Nothing about the candidacy or election of a member of
the clergy in any way endangers what this Supreme
Court ruling was attempting to achieve so far as the
separation of church and state is concerned.

The establishment clause is intended to prevent government from aiding or hindering religion, not to hinder
people of religious vocations from participating in the
government. The establishment is appropriately invoked
when there appears to be a danger that some sector of

government is favoring one religious tradition over another. It is a relevant consideration when religious symbols are injected into public places where persons of other traditions or no religious tradition at all might be offended.

In the June 23, 1998 edition of *The New York Times*, these questions receive attention on the front page of that esteemed newspaper. The ACLU is challenging the logo of the town of Republic, Missouri, because it bears the symbol of a fish, which is closely identified with the Christian faith. The question of keeping or removing that religious symbol became the major issue in the recent mayoral election, with the incumbent vowing to keep the symbol in the town seal. Laurie Goldstein writes in this article:

> Debates like this one in Republic over the separation of church and state are coming up with increasing regularity around the country. Sometimes the issue is a town's or state's logo or slogan with an explicitly religious reference, sometimes a crèche placed on public property, and sometimes a teacher or coach leading

students in prayer. Often, the conflicts
must be resolved in court.[7]

These are appropriate areas for the question of separation of church and state to be raised.

On that same day, June 23, 1998, *The Cleveland Plain Dealer* ran a similar story about prayer in public schools. To make the matter even more interesting than the case in Missouri, where the mayor was willing to defend the presence of a religious symbol in a town logo, in Alabama, Governor Fob James was the lead actor. He opposed a ruling by a local federal court that struck down an Alabama law that would have allowed "nonsectarian, nonproselytizing, student-initiated, voluntary prayers at all school related events...."[8] James appealed the judge's order to the 11th Circuit U.S. Court of Appeals, but then asked the Supreme Court to bypass the appeals court and order the federal judge to rescind his injunction. The Supreme Court rejected Governor James' appeal without comment.[9] This is another instance where the issue of separation of church and state is an important principle. In both Missouri and Alabama, however, the active agents were not members of the clergy who were pursuing a sectarian agenda. Instead, lay members of a Christian church were operating within their elective offices to press the issue. Political officials should be challenged when they attempt to hinder or assist a strictly religious issue. I would argue, however, that it is wrong to prevent a member of the clergy from serving in political office on the basis of the establishment clause, unless they engage in the kinds of maneuvers mentioned above. As has been shown, breaching the wall of separation is something that non-clergy political leaders are just as capable of doing as are members of the clergy, perhaps more so.

Rights and Responsibilities of the Clergy in the Church State Debate

The right of a member of the clergy to serve in public office is as deserving of protection as the right of the people to be protected from a governmental body, or from an over-reaching individual or institution, that seeks to determine if, how, or when people may engage in religious practices. This is especially the case if that clergyman has said or done nothing to suggest that he would use the political office to aid or hinder a religious agenda. Failure to safeguard this right is effectively to determine that a clergyman who holds public office is *guilty until proven innocent* of maintaining an appropriate neutrality on matters of religion.

Robert L. Maddox, in *Separation of Church and State: Guarantor of Religious Freedom*, points out those political actions that churches and ministers can and cannot engage in without endangering the church's tax exempt status with the Internal Revenue Service. In so doing, he shifts the focus away from the question of whether or not society must be shielded from a member of the clergy who, if elected to public office, may favor one religious tradition over another. Instead, he focuses on the economic impact that falls upon a congregation when it, or its clergy staff, behave inappropriately. After reviewing quite an extensive list of do's and don'ts,

Maddox concludes "churches can do more than they cannot." He suggests that churches can do such things as:

- Encourage voter registration and allow church facilities to be used by duly constituted voter registrars.

- Establish voter information forums and invite candidates to appear for question-and-answer sessions.

- Provide to candidates a list of church members that can be used to seek support in raising funds.

Maddox then lists some of the things that pastors can do. They include:

- Allow a candidate to use his name as a supporter or list him in political Advertisements.

- *Personally* endorse candidates for political office. (As an individual).

- Engage in lobbying in his individual capacity.

- Organize a Political Action Committee (PAC).

Next, he lists some of the things that cannot be done by the church or the minister:

- The church cannot endorse candidates for political office.

FROM PULPIT TO POLITICS

- The church cannot establish a PAC.

- The church cannot engage in substantial legislative activity.

The minister cannot endorse a political candidate (using the church's name).

Nowhere does Maddox suggest that a pastor should not seek office himself. He does list several things that ministers should not do, but they all have to do with using the political process to "impose their distinctive dogmas on the general population, or to see their theological doctrines imbedded in the civil law."[10] This is consistent with Carl Henry who states that "The church is not to use the mechanisms of government to legally impose upon society at large her theological commitments."[11]

There is absolutely no question that clergy should not seek political office in order to advance any denominational agenda or theological position. That point is well made by John C. Bennett, in his book, *Christians and the State*. Bennett writes:

> The churches in America should not use
> their members as political pressure
> groups to get special ecclesiastical privi-

leges for themselves as against other religious bodies. They should not seek legislation which interferes with the religious liberty of minorities and they should
be thankful that the courts stand guard at
this point.

No church, no matter how powerful,
should bring pressure on the state to enact
laws which are based upon principles that
depend for their validity on its own doctrine or ethos. It is wrong to make the
ethos of one part of the community the
basis of law.[12]

This is the area in which the separation of church and
state is meant to function, protecting the nation, and especially religious minorities, from the imposition of any
religious doctrine to which they must subscribe intel-
lectually or support financially. However, it has never
been the intent of the principle of separation of church
and state to prevent members of the clergy from seeking
or holding elective office. To do so, would deny to the
clergy one of the most basic rights of American citizenship.

FROM PULPIT TO POLITICS

Summary

What this chapter has argued, is that Jefferson's "wall of separation between church and state" has long since been breached, and members of the clergy are not the ones to be held most responsible. What is most needed at this point in time is to bring balance into the ways that religious values are being interpreted and applied to various matters of public policy. On issues such as abortion, homosexuality, capital punishment, euthanasia, birth control, war, nuclear weapons, the equal rights of women, vouchers for private and parochial schools, the teaching of creationism vs. evolution, and censorship vs. free speech, the voices of people speaking in the name of God are being heard on a regular basis. Based primarily upon their understanding of certain biblical teachings, some people from within the church are attempting, and with some success, to shape public policy in America.

The response to this fact is not to prevent clergy from serving in government on the spurious claim that such involvement violates the separation of church and state. The response is to require of all elected officials, lay and clergy alike, that they not use their public offices to aid or hinder any strictly religious issue or institution. Those ministers who have served in the U.S. Congress over the last fifty years, as well as those who have served at other levels of government, provide an immediate point of reference. They have all demonstrated an ability to serve their constituents and to represent the broad public interests, without becoming embroiled in issues or ideologies of a strictly religious nature. As mentioned, the list includes such persons as William Gray, Floyd Flake, Walter Fauntroy and Adam Clayton Powell, Jr., who continued to serve in their local churches while serving in the Congress.

I would suggest that the involvement of members of the clergy in the American political process has been beneficial. Clergy are intimately in touch with people at every level of society. Through their affiliation with local churches, whether as pastor or staff minister, they are

regularly accessible to people in the community. Their
position in the church makes them keenly aware of the
issues and concerns at work in the district they represent
in government. Most important of all, to deny them the
right to serve in public office merely because they are
clergy, with no evidence of wanting to pursue any issue
that would violate the separation of church and state, is
an infringement on a citizenship right that belongs to all
Americans.

Thus, I return to the comments from Robert McAfee
Brown mentioned at the beginning of this book:

> Any Christian worth his salt knows that
> in this day and age there is an imperative
> laid upon him to be politically responsi-
> ble. When one considers the fateful deci-
> sions which lie in the hands of the politi-
> cians, and the impact which these deci-
> sions will have for good or for ill upon
> the destinies of millions of people, it be-
> comes apparent that in terms of trying to
> implement the will of God, however
> fragmentarily, politics can be a means of
> grace. Christians may not retreat behind
> the specious excuse "politics is too

messy"; politics has become an area
where the most fastidious Christian must
act responsibly and decisively if he is not
to be derelict in his duties.[13]

The Religious Right has grasped this message and has
responded forcefully, not so much in terms of running
members of the clergy for elective office, but in actively
endorsing those political candidates who will support
them in advancing their social agenda.

Scriptural Sources That Inform Me

People should not allow themselves to be deterred
from acting politically by the notion that scripture sup-
ports a separation of church and state, based upon the
exchange between Jesus and the Sadduccees in Matthew
22: 17-21. During my congressional campaign, I was repeatedly confronted by the phrase: *Render unto Caesar
the things that are Caesar's, and unto God the things
that are God's.* This passage raises the question about
the legitimacy of paying taxes to the Roman government
during the years when Judea was a province within the

vast Roman Empire. Far from hinting that his followers should have nothing to do with the government, Jesus was urging all Judeans to render to the government those things owed by every citizen. That is the same point being made by Paul in Romans 13:7 when he says, *Render to all their dues: tribute to whom tribute is due.* Sherman E. Johnson, writing in *The Interpreters' Bible* observes that the phrase "render unto Caesar.....render unto God" means something very different depending upon the nature of the society in which one lives. He states:

> In a state like the Roman empire, where the subject had no political freedom, this may often be compatible with mere civil obedience. For a citizen in a free republic it involves intelligent and conscientious participation in politics so that God's will may be done as fully as possible.[14]

There is no biblical support for the notion that people of religious faith should not become actively involved in political life. Moreover, there are many biblical passages that point to the benefits that come to a society when it is

FROM PULPIT TO POLITICS

governed by those who acknowledge and seek to serve
God. None of those passages is more compelling than II
Samuel 23: 3-4 which says:
> He that ruleth over men must be just,
> ruling in the fear of God.
> And he shall be as the light of the morn-
> ing,
> when the sun riseth, even as a morning
> without clouds.

In Romans 13, Paul makes the case that government itself is established by God. How can Christians accept
the notion that they should not seek a role in that instrument which scripture teaches was established by God? I
am not suggesting that members of the clergy should be
the only ones to hold public office in American society.
However, there is no biblical basis for suggesting that a
member of the clergy is *prohibited* from holding a political office.

What remains is for persons of a broader, more moderate temperament, to step forward and join the political
process. Members of the clergy, black and white, must
be willing and able to answer this call to action. We

111

have much to offer. For those of us who are black, it is often the case that we are the persons best suited and best situated to step forward. For those who are white, it is no longer possible to contend that the church and state should be viewed as entirely separate spheres of influence. The fields of politics and public policy have already been targeted by the Religious Right. For more than a decade, they have seen these two areas as the arenas they must influence if they want to advance their agenda. I do not, by any means, begrudge them their aspiration. I simply believe that their perspective is often too narrow. The public debate about how church and state should interface during the coming years would be greatly served if the discussion could be broadened to include believers who are not limited to the agenda of the Religious Right. Members of the clergy with a broader, more informed understanding of what it means to be a socially and politically responsible Christian can make a significant contribution at precisely this point.

FROM PULPIT TO POLITICS

It seems clear that what is at stake is nothing less than the very definition of *who is a Christian* and *what constitutes authentic Christian faith?* Is Christianity only about Pro-Life issues, devoid of any consideration about family planning, poverty, sex education and the policies and funding that are needed to undergird these issues? Is there no room for a discussion about the inconsistency of being Pro-Life where birth is concerned, but rabidly pro-capital punishment where criminal justice is concerned? How shall we talk about developing a Pro-Family society that does not address providing sufficient medical care, decent housing, quality education and employment opportunities for all Americans?

Persons with Christian values must enter the political mainstream of this society informed by more than the simplistic pronouncements of the Christian Coalition, who believe that a war against a series of social issues ranging from abortion to divorce to the elimination of welfare programs can right what is wrong in American society. All of these are symptoms of the deeper sickness in our society. The real issues have not yet been addressed by the Religious Right or the Christian Coalition. Not until America stops focusing on symptoms, and starts addressing the real issues, will our society avoid any further conflicts or moral decline.

What Are the Issues for People of Biblical Faith?

The real issues are also deeply biblical and authentically Christian. They are addressed by the prophets of Israel and by Jesus. Authentic faith, says Amos 5:25, lets *justice roll down like water and righteousness like a mighty stream.* The prophet Isaiah says that the real issues are nothing less than *to loose the bands of wickedness, to undo the heavy burdens, to let the oppressed go free.., to deal thy bread to the hungry... and when thou seest the naked, that thou cover him* (Isaiah 58: 6-7). The real issues are addressed by Moses in Exodus 22 when he calls for a defense of *the widows, the orphans and the strangers within thy gates.*

FROM PULPIT TO POLITICS

The real issues are addressed by Jesus in the Great
Judgment scene in Matthew 25 when he says:
> I was hungry and you fed me,
>
> I was thirsty and you gave me drink,
>
> I was naked and you clothed me,
>
> I was sick and you cared for me,
>
> I was in prison and you visited me.
> And inasmuch as ye have done it unto the
> least of these my little ones, Ye have
> done it unto me.

Jesus points again to the real issues when he speaks at
the synagogue in Nazareth in Luke 4: 18-19 and de-
clares:
> The spirit of the Lord is upon me, be-
> cause he hath anointed me to preach the
> Gospel to the poor; he hath sent me to
> heal the broken-hearted, to preach deliv-
> erance to the captives, and recovering of
> sight to the blind, to set at liberty them
> that are bruised. To preach the acceptable
> year of the Lord.

If our nation is not led into an earnest discussion of these
issues, and if we do not provide policies and funds to
address these issues, it will matter very little that the

FROM PULPIT TO POLITICS

Religious Right wins or loses on the issues they have
identified.

Abortion, pornography, attacks on gays and lesbians,
and the absence of prayer in schools is not what ails our
nation most seriously. If all of these were resolved today,
we would still face a national crisis tomorrow. We
would still have to resolve issues of racism, sexism,
poverty and unemployment — due in part to corporate
down-sizing and the exporting of jobs to Third World
nations. We would still have to address under-funded
public schools, the free flow of illegal drugs into the
country, and a resurgent and recalcitrant gun lobby, now
headed by Charlton Heston, that fails to see the connection between the easy availability of hand guns and the
astounding rate of violent crime involving the use of
guns, ranging from robbery to battery to homicide.
Waving an American flag on the weekly program of a
tele-evangelist will not cause these critical problems to
go away. These are problems that demand an informed
electorate, an enlightened and responsive government,

FROM PULPIT TO POLITICS

and a commitment to policies and programs that can
bring healing and wholeness to our nation.

The present involvement of people of faith in
American political life is grossly unbalanced, with
members of the Religious Right and the Christian Coalition dominating not only the discussion, but the very
definition of who is a Christian and what is authentic
Christianity. It may be that the electorate is reluctant to
support the candidacy of a member of the clergy because
they fear that he or she might work only to advance the
concerns of conservative Christianity, without seeing the
broader and deeper issues that afflict the nation. The
need is for people who might be able to bring balance to
the discussion, and who might seek to represent their
faith more broadly than through the issues of Pro-Life or
Pro-Family, but also in terms of justice and equality and
opportunity in the world, as well as in the womb.

I agree with Jim Wallis who wrote in *Christianity
Today* that "the most important public policy question
that emerges from the Bible is how the poor, the vulner-

117

able, are being treated...Any organization that is calling itself Christian must have poor people and racial reconciliation on the agenda."[15]

Herein, I hope to sound the call to action, especially among members of my own profession, the clergy. It is hoped that some will feel called upon to respond. One thing is certain; there has never been a more urgent hour for members of the clergy to make the move *From Pulpit to Politics.*

Notes: Chapter Three

[1]Adriene Koch and William Rede. The Life and Selected Writings of Thomas Jefferson. (New York: The Modern Library, 1944) 333.

[2]Robert L. Maddox. Separation of Church and State. (New York: Crossroads, 1987) 94.

[3]Maddox 116.

[4]Koch, et al 335.

[5]Maddox 116.

[6]Stephen L. Carter. The Culture of Disbelief. (New York: Anchor Books, 1994) 110.

[7]Laurie Goodstein. "Town's logo becomes a religious battleground", The New York Times. 23 June 1998: 1A

[8]Richard Carrelli. "Alabama's appeal on prayer rejected", The Cleveland Plain Dealer. 23 June, 1998: 1A.

[9]Carrelli 1A.

[10]Maddox 158-161.

[11]Carl F.H. Henry. Christian Countermoves in a Decadent Culture. (Portland, OR: Multnomah Press, 1986) 118.

[12]John C. Bennett. Christians and the State. (New York: Scribners, 1958) 207.

[13]Robert McAfee Brown. "Confessions of a Political Neophyte", Christianity and Crisis, Volume XII 24, 19 Jan. 1953: 186.

[14]Sherman E. Johnson. "Matthew", The Interpreter's ✳ Bible Volume 7, (Nashville, TN: Abingdon Press, 1958) 520.

[15]John W. Kennedy. "Wild Card Election", Christianity Today, 26 Oct. 1998: 82.

FROM PULPIT TO POLITICS

Chapter Four: It Is Our Heritage

Any claim that by being actively involved in electoral politics means a black preacher is violating the principle of the separation between church and state must first be considered in light of the historic roles played by the black preacher over the last one hundred and fifty years. It must not be forgotten that the preacher represents the oldest model of political leadership in the black community. From the time of the Reconstruction to the present, no other person or group of persons in the black community has been as consistently involved in providing political leadership as the preacher.

The Emergence of the Preacher as the Leader in the Black Community

Many scholars have written and spoken of the leadership role of the black preacher in general terms without pointing to political leadership in particular. In 1903 W.E.B. Du Bois observed:

FROM PULPIT TO POLITICS

> The preacher is the most unique person-
> ality developed by the Negro on Ameri-
> can soil. A leader, a politician, an orator,
> a boss, an intriguer, an idealist...all these
> he is, and ever too, the centre of a group
> of men, now twenty, now one thousand in
> number. The combination of a certain
> adroitness with deep-seated earnestness,
> of tact with consummate ability, gave
> him his preeminence, and helps him
> maintain it.[1]

There were two reasons for the influence of the black
preacher by the turn of the twentieth century. The first
reason was the central role of the church in the black
community. It was at that point in time, and largely remains so to this day, the only major, social institution
wholly owned and operated by black people. The second
reason is the fact that a segregated society prohibited tal-
ented and ambitious black people from pursuing careers
in almost any other profession except the ministry.
Therefore, such people, with few other career opportunities, turned to the ministry and became leaders in the
most important institution in the black community.

FROM PULPIT TO POLITICS

A case can be made that the black preacher has been a significant leader within the community for more than one hundred and fifty years. Benjamin Quarles, in *Black Abolitionists* (1969), notes that this influence can be traced to the abolitionist movement of the 1840s, and for the same reason mentioned earlier. He says that the black clergy have great influence, because "colored men of other professions were in short supply."[2] He refers to correspondence between Martin Delany and Frederick Douglass, two significant non-clergy leaders of that era, in which Delany states, "As among our people generally in 1849, the church is the alpha and omega of all things."[3] Here, in the 1840s, are the two influences that resulted in the prestige attached to being a black preacher; the power and centrality of the church in the black community and the inaccessibility of other professional opportunities that resulted in people pursuing careers in ministry.

Kelly Miller, writing at the turn of the twentieth century, also joins these issues together in making a case

FROM PULPIT TO POLITICS

for the influence of the black preacher. Writing in *Out of the House of Bondage* (1910), Miller says:

> Within the church the opportunity for the talented tenth is almost unlimited. The Negro preacher has a larger influence and function than his white confrere, he is not only the spiritual adviser of his flock, but also their guide, philosopher, and friend. Almost every feature of leadership and authority comes within his prerogative.[4]

Careers outside of ministry were limited, but within the church one could gain not only employment, but prominence and some power within the community.

Writing in 1927, James Weldon Johnson, then serving as Executive Director of the NAACP, observed that "the Negro today is the most priest-governed group in the country."[5] Howard Brotz, in *Negro Social and Political Thought: 1850-1920*, writes that "The preacher was, even before the Civil War, the group leader of the Negro."[6] Leon Litwack, writing in *North of Slavery: The Negro in the Free States 1790-1860*, states:

> Indeed, the minister was unquestionably the most important and influential figure

> in the antebellum Negro community.
> While exercising a powerful political, so-
> cial, and moral influence, he also contrib-
> uted some of the most militant leadership
> to the Negro's struggle for human rights.[7]

These and other writers clearly acknowledge the promi-

nence and prestige enjoyed by the preacher, which for

this book serves as the basis for the political leadership

that many black preachers have exercised since Recon-

struction. Given the absence of leadership from any

other group, it was necessary that the black preachers

play a leadership role above and beyond the traditional

duties of pastoral care and spiritual formation.

A Brief Survey of Black Leaders Who Were Preachers

The Issue of Slavery

The influence of the black preacher has been felt in

a number of areas of public life beyond the traditional

work of preaching and serving the specific needs of a lo-

cal congregation. A Baptist minister named Nat Turner

FROM PULPIT TO POLITICS

led the bloodiest slave uprising in American history in Southampton County, Virginia in 1831.[8] An African Methodist Episcopal (AME) preacher named Morris Brown was forced to flee from Charleston, South Carolina in 1822 after his involvement in an attempted slave rebellion to be led by Denmark Vesey came to light. Brown went on to become a bishop in the AME church, and a college in Atlanta, Georgia is named after him.[9]

Benjamin Quarles points out that eight black people, all of them preachers, were listed among the founders of the American and Foreign Anti-Slavery Society in 1840[10]. Two of that group, Samuel Cornish and Henry Highland Garnet, became notable leaders for reasons beyond their involvement in the founding of the anti- slavery society. Cornish was also the co-founder, with John Russworm, of *The Freedom Journal*, the first black owned newspaper in the United States, which began publication in New York City in 1827.

In 1843, Garnet delivered a speech entitled, *"An Address to the Slaves of the United States"*, in which he called upon slaves across the South to rise up against their owners and gain their freedom through force of arms. Garnet, himself a fugitive slave from Maryland who had become a Presbyterian minister, gave this speech before an annual session of the Colored Convention, meeting that year in Buffalo, New York. The most famous section of that speech states:

> Let your motto be resistance! Resistance! Resistance! No oppressed people have ever secured their liberty without resistance....Rather die freemen than live to be slaves...If hereditary bondsmen would be free they themselves must strike the blow.[11]

This speech by Garnet was considered so provocative that the delegates to that convention, including Frederick Douglass, refused to adopt his statement as an official resolution. They feared that slave rebellions would erupt and be met with the kind of massive resistance from Southern state militia that occurred with the Nat Turner uprising in Virginia, in 1831.[12] Undeterred by that lack of support, Garnet managed to have his remarks made into a pamphlet that was circulated throughout the South by various anti-slavery groups. When John C. Calhoun, a United States Senator from South Carolina and a leader of the secessionist movement, gave reasons why secession might be necessary, he spoke about the effect of incendiary publications scattered over the whole South.[13] The 1843 pamphlet distributed by Garnet was among the earliest of those "incendiary publications".

The Colonization and Expatriation Movement

Henry Highland Garnet was not only a leader of the abolitionist movement, he also played a key role in the colonization movement which involved black Americans who left this country to establish new homes for themselves in various places in West Africa and the Caribbean.[14] Garnet was not the first black preacher to assume a leadership role in the colonization movement. In 1795, David George, a Baptist minister, led a group of freed slaves from Georgia to Nova Scotia to Sierra Leone.[15] Daniel Coker, one of the founders of the AME

Church in 1816, and the man initially selected to be that church's first bishop until he deferred in favor of Richard Allen, was also an early proponent of colonization. He migrated from Baltimore to Sierra Leone in 1820. Gayraud Wilmore, in *Black Religion and Black Radicalism* (1972), notes that Coker saw two distinct reasons for the colonization movement.

> Daniel Coker saw Negro colonization not only as a bid for independence and freedom for America's blacks, but as part of God's plan to bring the Christian faith to the land of his fathers through the ministry of the black church.[16]

This dual task of colonization and Christianization would be the primary work of a group called the African Colonization Society, of which Coker and Garnet were members.

Following Coker in immigrating to Africa both to colonize and Christianize was Lott Carey, a Baptist preacher from Richmond, Virginia, who led a group of émigrés to Sierra Leone and then to neighboring Liberia in 1821. Born a slave in 1790, Carey managed to purchase his freedom in 1813. He began his ministry in 1815 and quickly expressed a desire to join in the work of colonization and Christianization. He said:

> I am an African, and in this country, however meritorious my conduct, and respectable my character, I cannot receive the credit due to either. I wish to go to a country where I shall be esteemed by my merits, not by my complexion; and I feel bound to labor for my suffering race.[17]

As founder and first president of the African Civilization Society, Garnet would echo the sentiments of both Coker and Carey when he writes, "…we hold it to be the duty of the Christian and the philanthropist in America, either to send or carry the Gospel and civilization to Africa."[18]

As a way of continuing his assault against slavery in the United States, Garnet added another dimension to the concepts of colonization and Christanization. He envisioned the development of a cotton industry in Liberia that would not only provide the basis for an economy for the infant colony, but that same cotton would be produced and sold at a lower price than could be matched by growers in the United States. The creation of a new and cheaper source of cotton would serve consumers throughout the United States and Europe who did not want to support a slave economy, but who needed a reliable source for cotton. In so doing, it would have dealt a serious blow to the profitability and thus the viability of slavery in the United States. The plan was never implemented, however, because of the outbreak of the Civil War.[19]

Thus far, we have examined the lives of Samuel Cornish, Henry Highland Garnet, Daniel Coker and Lott Carey, black preachers who were deeply involved in the public affairs of the antebellum era. I would suggest that these men prepared the way for the more overt political activism of the black preachers in the generations that followed.

FROM PULPIT TO POLITICS
Civil War and Reconstruction Era

Let me turn next to three black preachers of the Civil War and Reconstruction era whose careers did turn not only to activism around public policy, but took on a decidedly political focus. The first is Henry McNeil Turner. He was an AME, who became the first black man ever named to be an Army chaplain, serving the all-black regiments of the Union Army following his appointment by Abraham Lincoln in 1864.[20] Following the Civil War, Turner became active in Republican Party politics in Georgia, and was elected to the Georgia State Legislature in 1868.[21] John Dittmer wrote, concerning Turner's influence, "At thirty-three, Turner was the most influential religious and political leader in Georgia, the state with the largest black population."[22]

Daniel Payne, who would become an AME bishop, was also the first black college president in the United States when he assumed the presidency of Wilberforce College, in Ohio, in 1856. This was the first college in American history to be owned and operated by black

FROM PULPIT TO POLITICS

people when it was organized by the AME church.
However, Payne was also an abolitionist leader who
took his case directly to the President of the United
States when he met with Abraham Lincoln in the White
House on April 14, 1862.

Payne met with Lincoln to urge the President to sign
a bill that would abolish slavery in the District of Columbia which was, at that time, home to over three thou-
sand slaves. With so many slaves residing in the nation's
capitol, Payne accused Lincoln of being one of the biggest slave owners in the United States. According to
Benjamin Quarles, "two days after Payne's visit Lincoln
signed the bill."[23] This was the first time any black person had ever been granted a private audience with the
President of the United States. Thus, a black preacher
was operating at the highest level of American political
life over one hundred and thirty years ago. No one at that
time, or since, has accused Payne of violating the principle of separation of church and state.

133

FROM PULPIT TO POLITICS

The most important black preacher of the nineteenth century, insofar as the move from pulpit to politics is concerned, was Hiram Revels. He, too, was an AME preacher, who began his career as a recruiter for two of the all-black regiments of the Union Army from Missouri and Maryland. In 1869, following one term in the Mississippi State Legislature, Revels would be appointed to a vacant seat in the United States Senate, becoming the first black person, and still one of only three black people, ever to serve in that body. Ironically, he would fill the seat vacated by Jefferson Davis, who had resigned from the Senate in order to become President of the Confederate States of America.[24]

Turner and Revels were not the only black preachers who held political office in the years after the Civil War. Many other black preachers were also political office holders during the Reconstruction period. The Rev. Richard Cain served two terms in the United States House of Representatives from South Carolina between 1873-1875 and 1877-1879. Eric Foner, in *A Short His-*

134

tory of Reconstruction (1986), writes, "every AME preacher in Georgia was said to be active in Republican Party organizing, and political materials were read aloud at churches."[25] Foner quotes The Rev. Charles H. Pearce of Florida, who said, "A man in this state cannot do his whole duty as a minister except he looks out for the political interests of his people."[26] Foner continues:

> Even those preachers who lacked ambition for political position sometimes found it thrust upon them. Often among the few literate blacks in a community, they were called upon to serve as election registrars and candidates for office. Over 100 black ministers would be elected to legislative seats during Reconstruction.[27]

When the Reconstruction era ended as a result of various political maneuvers and massive amounts of physical intimidation, black voting rights were quickly curtailed and black elected officials disappeared from all state and federal positions. However, the leadership role of the black preacher continued and became all the more important. James Washington, in *Frustrated Fellowship:*

FROM PULPIT TO POLITICS

The Black Quest for Social Power, quotes The Rev. Walter Brooks who said in 1892:

> Our political leaders are few, and even those we have cannot reach the people, therefore, it becomes our duty to speak out upon all questions that effect our people socially, economically, as well as religiously.[28]

To this point, I have demonstrated that black preachers have served in the role of elected officials dating as far back as 1869, making the black preacher the longest continuing model of political leadership. Even when black political power was all but eliminated during the Post-Reconstruction era, especially after the 1880s, black preachers remained the only group able to provide leadership for black people in America. This period of repression and intimidation was referred to by the novelist, Charles Chestnutt, as "the nadir", or the darkest and lowest period of the history of blacks in this country.[29]

FROM PULPIT TO POLITICS

The Leadership Role of the Black Teacher

It should be noted that during this same period another leadership group did begin to emerge, the black schoolteacher. To some degree, the black preacher has functioned in this teaching role as well, especially in the context of the historically black colleges and universities. Such persons as Mordecai Johnson at Howard University, Benjamin E. Mays at Morehouse College, and Samuel D. Proctor at Virginia Union University and North Carolina A&T University, were black preachers who served as college and university presidents.

However, the black school teacher, especially in the South, emerged alongside that black preacher as a significant leadership group. Still, there were some certain factors that prevented the leadership of the black teacher from being as effective as it might have been. In his study, *The Education of Blacks in the South: 1860-1935,* James Anderson demonstrates that black teachers did experience a form of vulnerability from which the black preacher was somewhat insulated. Black teachers were usually paid by the state or county governments, which were controlled by whites. Black schools could be closed down so that those students were available to work in the agricultural industries during the time of the harvest. While the black teacher was an invaluable resource in local communities across the country, the institutions in which they worked were neither owned or controlled by that local black community. Black teachers often worked at the whim and discretion of the white political establishment. This fact made the teacher vulnerable in ways that did not effect the black preacher.

Kelly Miller writes about that vulnerability when he says:

> The Negro preacher will be the spokesman of the people, because his support comes directly from them. The teacher, on the other hand, whose stipend is controlled by the officers of the state, dares indulge in only such utterances as will not displease those upon whose good graces his tenure of place depends.[30]

The best example of this involves Septima Clark, a leading figure of the Civil Rights Movement of the

FROM PULPIT TO POLITICS

1950s and 1960s. In 1956, after decades as a public school teacher in South Carolina, her contract was not renewed by the school board where she was employed, because she refused to renounce the NAACP or promise to disassociate herself from its activities.[31]

Similarly, when the sit-ins involving black college students across the South began to occur in 1960, many black college presidents found themselves facing a dilemma. Should they support their students who were risking their lives in pursuit of a just society, or should they discourage that pursuit in order to safeguard their college's annual allocation from the state legislature? It was because of their vulnerability to that kind of reprisal from whites that Aldon Morris writes, "Rather than support the movement, therefore, many of the teachers and administrators attempted to block it from taking root on their campuses."[32]

FROM PULPIT TO POLITICS

Key Ingredients in the Leadership Role of the Black Preacher

It is precisely because many black preachers have been insulated from economic reprisal from white society that their leadership status has been able to continue. Consider that during the time when educators were being intimidated by the threat of the loss of a job at the elementary and secondary levels, and with a cut in state funding at the college level, black preachers like Martin Luther King, Jr., Andrew Young, Ralph Abernathy, and many others were leading massive demonstrations across the South. These ministers could be threatened and harassed by white city officials and by groups like the Ku Klux Klan. However, they could not be summarily disciplined or dismissed by white society, because they were employed by members of all-black churches or church-based organizations that believed in and supported the work they were doing.

FROM PULPIT TO POLITICS

Writing about life in Chicago in the 1920s and 1930s in *Black Metropolis: A Study of Negro Life in a Northern City*, Horace Clayton and St. Clair Drake noted:

> Negro preachers have the greatest freedom of any race leaders. Politicians must fit themselves into machine politics. Most civic leaders are dependent upon white philanthropy. Most of Bronzeville's preachers are answerable to no one except their congregation. They can say what they please about current affairs and race relations. There are no church superiors to discipline them and no white people to take economic reprisal.[33]

Writing from the perspective of the 1970s, Charles V. Hamilton notes, in *The Black Preacher in America*, that black preachers remain the only leadership group in the community who enjoy economic insulation from any form of reprisal by white society. Moreover, the black preacher also enjoys an institutional base that can be tapped and mobilized without seeking permission from, or paying a fee to, white society; namely the network of local churches. Hamilton observes:

> The black lawyer, the black labor leader,
> the black politician — all these people
> are growing in number in the black com-
> munity. But until they develop pervasive,
> indigenous black organizational struc-
> tures, they will have to rely heavily on the
> black preachers for help in reaching and
> mobilizing the masses.[34]

Other groups have emerged to share the leadership responsibility with the black preacher. However, they lack
two ingredients, long enjoyed by the preacher, without
which leadership is difficult to exert. The first is regular
access to masses of people who gather to hear what he or
she has to say. The other is buildings and facilities where
meetings can be held, where information can be produced and distributed, and where issues can be discussed. Until black leaders in other professions can meet
these two criteria, the importance of the preacher as a
leader in the community will not be eclipsed.

FROM PULPIT TO POLITICS

The Black Church as a Political Arena

In the congressional campaign in 1998, people objected to my candidacy on the basis of separation of church and state. Yet, those same people were not disturbed by the attempts by all three major candidates in my race, and dozens of other candidates seeking other offices, to appear before as many black church groups as possible in order to appeal for their votes. One edition of *The Cleveland Plain Dealer* was devoted to which black pastors and black clergy groups were endorsing which congressional candidates. In that article, Jeffrey Johnson is quoted as saying, "You seek as many ministers' blessings as possible. You literally seek each minister."[35] Another edition of that same newspaper devoted its Monday morning front page to the campaigning of congressional candidates in black churches on the Sunday preceding the primary election.[36] So intense was the campaigning within black churches that an edition of *The Sun Press*, a smaller community newspaper, ran a cartoon of a black pastor standing in the pulpit of his church which was strewn with campaign banners, saying: "O.K., may I now have my church back?"[37]

The focus by political candidates on campaigning in as many black churches as possible, and on gaining the support of black preachers, is consistent with an observation made by Charles V. Hamilton. He comments that when a person in New York City was planning to seek a certain office in that city, the first advice he was given was "Get to the ministers!"[38] It is important to note that not all black preachers are politically active, nor do they all allow political candidates to appear in their churches. Katherine Tate, in her book, *From Protest to Politics*, suggests that:

> Blacks who belonged to activist churches were more likely to vote regularly and to participate in campaign activities...The percentage of core voters was far higher among Blacks who belonged to churches where political participation was encouraged...Far from representing an anti-political agency, the church continues to serve as a vital link to politics within the Black community.[39]

Thus, part of the challenge of campaigning in the black community is identifying those churches and pastors who are open to allowing candidates to appear. When such places are identified and the invitation to come is extended, the results can be decisive for an aspiring political candidate. Not every church or every pastor is involved in politics, but every candidate who runs is anxious to campaign in those churches that are politically active.

It is inconsistent at best, and perhaps hypocritical, for voters, candidates, and political organizations to actively seek out and involve black preachers and black churches in the campaigns of other candidates, but point to the separation of church and state when the preacher seeks to become the candidate. If it is wrong for the preacher to move beyond the church and seek political office, why is it right for non-clergy persons seeking political office to attempt to be introduced and to actively campaign inside the church? Either the black church

FROM PULPIT TO POLITICS

must be a political Free-Zone, or it must be an arena in which both lay and clergy alike can be actively engaged.

In far too many instances, the campaign season is the only time that some politicians show any interest in the church or the clergy. They court you and reassure you as to how important the church and the clergy are when they want to come into the church to be elected or re-elected. But when the church calls upon them for assistance after they have been elected, some of them can be hard to find. This does not happen when the preacher is elected to public office, because the preacher remains institutionally connected to, and is regularly accessible to the community through the local church. Even those who serve in political offices that require them to travel to the state or national capitol, return to the district every week- end. The real problem resides with too many non-clergy politicians who exploit the church during election season, and then ignore the church, the pastors, and their issues until the next campaign rolls around.

146

FROM PULPIT TO POLITICS

It is my contention that in the black church the bridge between the pulpit and politics was spanned over one hundred and fifty years ago. This activist role has allowed hundreds of black preachers to cross over into various roles of active political leadership. It has also allowed thousands of non-clergy politicians to come into the black church and present their qualifications and reasons for running for public office. Claims of separation of church and state ring hollow when directed against a black preacher who is running for public office. That is because black preachers have been serving in public office at every level of government since Hiram Revels served in the United States Senate from Mississippi in 1869.

Four Models of Leadership among Black Preachers

The argument that a black preacher serving in a political office is a violation of the separation of church and state is further refuted by Peter Paris in his book, *Black Religious Leaders*. In that book, Paris argues that black preachers have historically operated out of four models of leadership. The one that is most familiar, and the model from which most black preachers operate, he calls the *priestly* model. This model involves the preacher in the traditional tasks of pastoral care. Paris traces the roots of this model back to the slave preachers of the antebellum era, who could not dramatically effect the condition of their people during slavery. Instead, they attempted to comfort and console their congregations. Paris says, "Priests helped people to endure things they could not readily change, and to make constructive use of every opportunity for self-development under the conditions of bondage."[40]

Paris is quite explicit about the fact that those operating out of the priestly mode are not likely to engage in any form of social or political agitation against any of the conditions that confront them. Instead, they are likely to be found "helping people accommodate themselves to those conditions of racism without affirming those conditions."[41] This is consistent with the historical record.

FROM PULPIT TO POLITICS

In the same essay in which Du Bois mentions the pre-
eminence of the black preacher, he also speaks about the
earliest role that the black preacher played in the slave
community. He places the roots of the black preacher in
the West African medicine man or priest who arrived in
the Americas as part of the Trans- Atlantic slave trade.
Du Bois says:

> He early appeared on the plantation and
> found his function as the healer of the
> sick, the interpreter of the Unknown, the
> comforter of the sorrowing, the super-
> natural avenger of wrong, and the one
> who rudely but picturesquely expressed
> the longing, disappointment, and resent-
> ment of a stolen and oppressed people.
> Thus as bard, physician, judge and priest,
> within the narrow limits allowed by the
> slave system, rose the Negro preacher,
> and under him the first Afro-American
> institution, the Negro church.[42]

Other roles would soon evolve, but the first role filled by
the black preacher is what Paris calls the priestly model
of leadership.

FROM PULPIT TO POLITICS

The second type of leadership mentioned by Paris is the *prophetic* model. In describing this type of leadership, Paris writes, "The prophetic style is characterized by the principle of criticism. Prophets are reformers. They never accommodate themselves to the status quo."[43] Central to this style of leadership is that society itself, and not any particular individual, is the target of one's energies. The intent of the prophet is to alter existing public policies either through moral suasion or protest. Rather than being limited to the life of the congregation, the black preacher as prophet engages in direct lobbying and agitation with political, business and media leaders. Martin Luther King, Jr. coined a phrase for this kind of ministry when he said that the purpose of his organization, the Southern Christian Leadership Conference, was "to save the soul of America."[44] Very few people that I have encountered have attempted to suggest that King and the other black preachers involved in the Civil Rights Movement were in violation of the principle of separation of church and state. Yet, it was their expressed purpose to influence and alter the domestic and foreign policy agenda of this nation during the 1950s and 1960s.

The third model of leadership as defined by Paris is *nationalistic.* Typified by such people as Malcolm X, and now Louis Farrakhan, leaders operating out of this model are essentially separatists. Paris says:

> This type is convinced that the society
> lacks the capacity for repentance, since it
> is viewed as morally decadent to the core.
> Evil is thought to be endemic; pervading
> every dimension of the society's
> life...This type calls on its followers to
> dis-associate themselves completely from
> the society and to set themselves to con-
> structing a new society that bears no trace
> of the old.[45]

Those operating out of this leadership model are not likely to be charged with violating separation of church and state lines since separation from society is what they advocate.

The fourth model of leadership offered by the black preacher is what Paris calls the *political* model. Tracing

the roots of this model back to the Reconstruction era,
Paris says, "This type of leadership is goal oriented and
unafraid of compromise. It prefers to obtain a portion of
its goal rather than none, and is the most pragmatic of all
our ideal types."[46] Paris uses Adam Clayton Powell, Jr.
as the best example of this model of clergy leadership.
This is the historical model out of which I was operating
when I ran for Congress. Having worked as an Associate
Pastor of Abyssinian Baptist Church in New York from
1972-1976 under Powell's successor, Dr. Samuel Dewitt
Proctor, my basic understanding of ministry has always
included an appreciation for this *political* model. This is
the historical model that validates the aspirations of any
black preacher who runs for public office. It is less than
convincing to charge a black preacher who is seeking
public office with violating the principle of separation of
church and state in light of this historical model identified by Peter Paris.

    While Paris uses the career of Adam Clayton Powell,
Jr., as the personification of the black preacher as politi-

cal leader, we cannot overlook the fact that there is an even more recent example of a black preacher who, even in defeat, made great use of the *political* model of leadership. I am referring to the 1984 and 1988 Presidential campaigns of the Rev. Jesse Jackson. This Baptist preacher, who has been active in Civil Rights issues since his student days at North Carolina A.&T., and who stood with Dr, Martin Luther King, Jr., right up until the day he was assassinated, became a major force in Democratic Party politics as a result of his two Presidential campaigns. Jackson was elected a non- voting member of the U.S. Senate from the District of Columbia in 1990.

Black Preachers in Congress in the 20th Century

It is often overlooked that seven black preachers have served in the United States Congress within the last thirty years. Adam Clayton Powell, Jr. served from 1944-1968, rising to become Chairman of the House Education and Labor Committee. Andrew Young ,who represented a district encompassing Atlanta, Georgia from 1972-1976, followed Powell. Young went on to serve as United States Ambassador to the United Nations under President Jimmy Carter. He later served two terms as Mayor of Atlanta, and ran for Governor of Georgia in 1990. William Gray represented a district in Philadelphia, Pennsylvania from 1978-1992. He became Chairman of the House Budget Committee and House Majority Whip. All the while, he continued as pastor of Bright Hope Baptist Church of Philadelphia.

Walter Fauntroy, Chairman of the Board of the Southern Christian Leadership Conference, and pastor of the New Bethel Baptist Church of Washington, D.C., was also the non-voting representative from the District of Columbia to the U.S. House of Representatives from 1971-1991. Floyd Flake served as pastor of Allen Temple AME Church in Jamaica, Queens, New York, and served in Congress from 1986-1997. John Lewis of Georgia and J.C. Watts of Oklahoma are both ordained ministers and members of Congress. In light of the history of the black preacher as politician, and in light of these men who have, or do serve in the United States Congress, there is no substance to the claim that the candidacy of a minister is necessarily a violation of the principle of the separation of church and state.

It is important to note that black preachers have served not only in the Congress, but at the state and local levels as well. Here is a list of some of the black preachers whom I have known personally, and who have served in elected or appointed political positions, outside of Congress, over the last fifty years. Gardner C. Taylor, pastor emeritus of Concord Baptist Church of Brooklyn, New York, served as a member of the New York City Board of Education. Sandy F. Ray, most noted for his years as pastor of Cornerstone Baptist Church of Brooklyn, New York, served in the Ohio Legislature during the years when he served a pastorate in Columbus, Ohio. Michael Haynes served in the Massachusetts legislature, and later on the State Pardon and Parole Board in the 1970s. S. Howard Woodson was the senior member of the New Jersey legislature while remaining the pastor of Shiloh Baptist Church of Trenton. J. Archibald Carey served in the Illinois legislature, and later was a Chicago Alderman while he was the pastor of Quinn Chapel AME Church of Chicago. Matthew Carter served as Mayor of Montclair, New Jersey. Leonidas B. Young served as Mayor of Richmond, Virginia, and continues to serve in City Council while serving as pastor of Fourth Baptist Church. Samuel Proctor directed the Peace Corps in Nigeria during the Kennedy administration, and the Office of Economic Opportunity under President Lyndon Johnson.

Closer to home, in the Greater Cleveland area, four black Baptist ministers have served as school board presidents in neighboring districts in recent time: David Hunter in East Cleveland, Steven Sullivan and Hilton Smith in Cleveland, and I serve in that same capacity in Shaker Heights. E.T. Caviness was a member of Cleveland City Council and later worked on the staff of then Cleveland Mayor George Voinovich. He is now the

Chairman of the Ohio Civil Rights Commission. Nathaniel Bolden is a Democratic Party ward leader in Warrensville Heights. Tyrone Bolden served on Cleveland City Council. Sterling Glover is Chairman of the Port Authority. Albert Rowan served on the City of Cleveland Planning Commission. Otis Moss, Jr. co-chaired the process that resulted in the mayoral take-over of the Cleveland public schools, and Larry Harris was a member of that committee. All of these men are black preachers.

Given the number of black preachers who have been elected or appointed to political office throughout Cuyahoga County, the suggestion that my campaign for Congress was a violation of the principle of separation of church and state was surprising. Is there some assumption that a clergy person running for a local office is acceptable, while running for a federal office is not? Or did people simply not realize how many black preachers have served in political offices all across the

11th Congressional district and all across the country, dating back to Reconstruction?

The Future of the Black Preacher in Politics

One thing may have changed since Reconstruction, so far as the political activity of the black preacher is concerned. Carter G. Woodson, in his book *The History of the Negro Church*, devotes an entire chapter to the subject *"The Call of Politics."* He reminds the reader once again that the preacher had to become involved in politics, because he was the only member of the black community positioned at that time to perform such a role. Woodson says:

> There were during the Reconstruction period, moreover, so many necessities with which the Negroes had to be supplied that the Negro preacher, often the only one in their community sufficiently well grounded in the fundamentals to lead them, had to devote his time not only to church work but to every matter of concern to the race.[47]

FROM PULPIT TO POLITICS

In short, black preachers initially got involved in politics because there were not enough people of other professions in the community able to fill all of the leadership positions that were opening up in the years following the Civil War, especially after the passage of the 15th Amendment that gave black people the right to vote.

That is no longer the case. Preachers are no longer the only pool of candidates from which leadership roles can be filled. Blacks have now moved in great numbers into the fields of business and law, fields from which white society has long drawn its political leaders. More will be said about this, and about why white preachers have not emerged as political leaders within their communities, in the next chapter. Increasingly, black political leaders have been coming from those arenas of activity. In my race for Congress, the incumbent and both of my major opponents were lawyers.

If a black preacher seeks election to a political office at this point in time, it is not so much because no one is able or available from any other sector of the community. Often, it is a simple matter of a combination of ability, aspiration and opportunity on the part of the preacher. It is no longer a matter of the community turning to the black preacher because there is no one else to whom they can turn. Instead, it is more likely a matter of the preacher being willing to contend against others for political office, because he or she sees in that office an opportunity to influence and shape polices and events in ways that are not possible when one remains entirely within the pulpit. It is a way of "making politics a means of grace", as Robert McAfee Brown suggested almost fifty years ago.

Things have changed somewhat over the last one hundred and twenty-five years insofar as leadership in the black community is concerned. However, so long as black people remain even slightly marginalized in American society, and so long as the church remains the central institution owned and operated by black people, black preachers will continue to be an active and formidable political force in the community. This will still

FROM PULPIT TO POLITICS

happen, simply because of the preacher's leadership role in the black church, and the church's leadership role in the black community.

The reporter who covered the congressional primary campaign in the 11th District of Ohio during the Spring of 1998 acknowledged that the black church was the primary arena in which that campaign was conducted. Joe Hallett wrote about that in the days following the May 5th primary. He said:

> In a district that is 60 percent black, the
> campaign largely played out in black
> churches, where the level of political dis-
> course in a series of debates was higher
> than any I had ever heard.[48]

The leadership role played by the black preacher will not be the political model, in most instances. The priestly and prophetic roles will remain the dominant models. And many black preachers may choose to be politically active by hosting candidate forums or speaking on political issues, as I mentioned in the Preface. But when a black preacher does decide to seek elective office, those efforts cannot be challenged on historical,

FROM PULPIT TO POLITICS

constitutional or biblical grounds. The political model of ministry for black preachers reaches back to Reconstruction. There is no reason why it should not be allowed to reach forward into the 21st century. I contend that the need still exists for some black preachers to move *From Pulpit to Politics.*

Notes: Chapter Four

[1]W.E.B. Du Bois. The Souls of Black Folk. (Greenwhich, CN: Fawcett Books) 141.

[2]Benjamin Quarles. Black Abolitionists. (New York: Da Capo Press, 1969) 69.

[3]Quarles 69.

[4]Kelly Miller. Out of the House of Bondage. (New York: Schocken Books, 1971) 203-204.

[5]James Weldon Johnson. God's Trombones. (New York: Viking Press, 1969) 3.

[6]Howard Brotz, ed. Negro Social and Political Thought. (New York: Basic Books, 1966) 526.

[7]Leon Litwack. North of Slavery: The Negro in the Free States 1790-1860. (University of Chicago Press, 1961) 187.

[8]Leon Litwack. Black Leaders of the Nineteenth Century. (Urbana: University of Illinois Press, 1991) 26-36.

[9]Carter G. Woodson. History of the Negro Church. (Washington, D.C.: The Association Press, 1972) 67.

[10]Quarles 68.

[11]Earl Ofari. Let Your Motto Be Resistance. (Boston: Beacon Press, 1972) 153.

[12]Ofari 38-39.

[13]John L. Thomas. Slavery Attacked: The Abolitionist Crusade. (Englewood Cliffs, NJ: Prentice Hall, 1965) 53-54.

[14]Brotz 191.

[15]Woodson 116.

[16]Gayraud Wilmore. Black Religion and Black Radicalism. (Garden City, NJ: Anchor Books, 1972) 143.

[17]Leon Fitts. Lott Carey: First Black Missionary to Africa. (Valley Forge, PA: Judson Press, 1978) 27.

[18]William Jeremiah Moses. The Golden Age of Black Nationalism. (New York: Oxford, 1978) 38.

[19]Litwack 143.

[20]Litwack 255.

[21]Litwack 257.

[22]Litwack 257.

[23]Benjamin Quarles. The Negro and the Civil War. (New York: Da Capo Press, 1989) 139.

[24]"Jefferson Davis", Webster's American Biographies. (Springfield, MA: G. and C. Merriam Co., 1974) 257.

[25]Eric Foner. A Short History of Reconstruction. (New York: Norton, 1989) 41.

[26]Foner 41.

FROM PULPIT TO POLITICS

[27]Foner 41.

[28]James M. Washington. Frustrated Fellowship: The Baptist Quest for Social Power. (Macon, GA: Mercer University Press, 1986) 158.

[29]C. Vann Woodward. The Strange Career of Jim Crow. (New York: Oxford, 1973) 96.

[30]Miller 213.

[31]Aldon E. Morris. Origins of the Civil Rights Movement. (New York: The Free Press, 1984) 139.

[32]Morris 196.

[33]St. Clair Drake and Horace Clayton. Black Metropolis: A Study of Negro Life in a Northern City. (University of Chicago Press, 1945) 427.

[34]Charles V. Hamilton. The Black Preacher in America. (New York: Morrow, 1972) 221-222.

[35]Joel Hallett. "Candidates seek black ministers' support", The Cleveland Plain Dealer 29 April 1998: 1A.

[36]Joe Hallett, "Storming the Churches", The Cleveland Plain Dealer, 3 May 1998: 1A.

[37]The Sun Press, 9 May 1998: A4.

[38]Hamilton 13.

[39]Katherine Tate. From Protest to Politics. (Cambridge, MA: Harvard, 1993) 95.

[40]Peter Paris. Black Religious Leaders. (Louisville, KY: Westminster/John Knox Press, 1991) 19.

[41]Paris 19.

[42]Du Bois 142.

[43]Paris 20.

[44]Adam Farclough. To Redeem the Soul of America. (Athens: University of Georgia, 1987).

[45]Paris 23.

[46]Paris 22.

[47]Woodson 198-223.

[48]Joe Hallett. "11th District Race Was Too Clean to See", The Cleveland Plain Dealer, 8 May 1998: 11B.

FROM PULPIT TO POLITICS

Chapter Five: It Is Our World

The issue of separation of church and state is no less intense within the white community, and especially within the conservative, white evangelical church. The lines that mark the boundaries between the pulpit and politics have become more obscured than ever, as both preachers and politicians cross them in pursuit of their respective goals. The June 14, 1998 edition of *The New York Times*, observed that seven of the most powerful political leaders in the United States are active members of the Southern Baptist Convention, an increasingly conservative and politically active group in American life. They are President Bill Clinton, Vice President Al Gore, House Speaker Newt Gingrich, and Senate Majority Leader Trent Lott. One can add to that list the names of Strom Thurmond, who is President Pro-Temp of the Senate, Tom Delay, the House Majority Leader and Richard Gephardt, the House Minority Leader.[1]

FROM PULPIT TO POLITICS

The Influence of the Religious Right

Senator Trent Lott was prominent in the June16,
1998 issue of *The New York Times*, giving his views on
such controversial issues as abortion, the respective roles
of husbands and wives in marriage and homosexuality,
which he explicitly referred to as "a sin".[2] As reported in
the June 15, 1998 edition of *USA Today*, nine contenders
for the Republican Party's presidential nomination in the
year 2000 addressed a group of party faithful in Cedar
Rapids, Iowa, the sight of the nation's first presidential
primaries. Steve Forbes was quoted as saying to this political gathering, "It's time we stopped being ashamed of
speaking God's name from public platforms in America."[3] Representative John Kasich of Ohio said, "God
has given us a road map...[4] Jill Lawrence notes that:

> Here in Iowa, the Christian Coalition is
> so intertwined with the State party that its
> lunch Saturday featuring Oliver North
> was listed as an official convention event.
> Fully 40% of the participants in Iowa's
> first-in-the-nation presidential nominat-
> ing caucuses are Christian activists.[5]

FROM PULPIT TO POLITICS

Christopher Caldwell, writing in *The Atlantic Monthly*, notes that the Republican Party may be identifying too closely with "the Christian right." He says, "The party is trying to impose the folkways of one regional subculture on the whole country."[6]

Laurie Goodstein does note that the political leaders who share a membership in the Southern Baptist Convention do not necessarily agree on all issues. But the fact remains that it is becoming increasingly difficult to win an election, especially as a Republican candidate, without seeking the support of, and endorsing the social agenda of conservative Christian groups. While candidates are seeking the support of conservative religious groups, many candidates are also turning to Ralph Reed, formerly the head of The Christian Coalition and now a political campaign consultant, to help them shape a campaign that will be acceptable to conservative Christian voters.

> Among his twenty seven clients are "three candidates for governor, two for the U.S. Senate, eight for the House of Representatives and six for lesser state-

wide offices....Reed speaks regularly to
five prospective Republican presidential
candidates...four of whom have expressed an interest in retaining his
firm....One of his existing clients, Mitch
Skandalakis who is running for Lieuten-
ant Governor of Georgia said about his
choice of Reed as his campaign consultant, obviously we wanted someone who
has credibility with the religious right and
can say with 100 percent certainty that
the guy he's supporting shares their message and values.[7]

Has there ever been a time when the lines between
church and state have ever been more blurred than they
are right now?

It seems shortsighted that people could oppose the
political aspirations of a member of the clergy on separation grounds, given what is actually happening in the
country today. It is not likely that the influence of conservative Christianity on American politics is going to
be diminished any time soon, especially on the national
level. The wisest course of action may not be to discourage the clergy from running for office, but to see in their

election an opportunity to offer a broader, more informed and more balanced view on the social-religious questions that currently occupy center stage in the national political debate.

The genie is now out of the bottle. To speak about maintaining a separation between church and state as if the Christian Coalition, the Southern Baptist Convention and other conservative, evangelical groups have not already laid claim to the Republican Party and did not already greatly influence the present political landscape in America, is totally naïve. It is no longer a question of whether or not religious leaders, lay and clergy, should participate in American politics. The only question left to be answered is whether the more conservative forces, typified by such persons as Jerry Falwell, Pat Robertson and D. James Kennedy, will be the only ones to put forward both an agenda and a slate of candidates. At present, that seems to be the case. My decision to seek a seat in the U.S. Congress was greatly influenced by my desire to be able to stand against their understanding of what are the issues that should most concern the congress and the country at the turn of the 21st century.

From the Moral Majority to the Christian Coalition

The bridge between the pulpit and politics in the conservative, white church in America, was spanned by such white preachers as Falwell, Robertson and Kennedy almost twenty years ago. Falwell was the founder of The Moral Majority, a 1970s and 1980s group that actually laid the foundations for what later became the "religious right." Pat Robertson, founder and host of the nationally televised *The 700 Club* and the owner of *The Family Channel* which broadcasts family-oriented programs on cable stations across the country, sought the Republican Party presidential nomination in 1984 and 1988. D. James Kennedy is one of a host of tele-evangelists whose national broadcasts are so peppered with references to the American flag and to "winning America for Christ" rhetoric that the viewer wonders where Kennedy sees the line between patriotism and partisan religious evangelization.

James C. Dobson, a leading member of the Christian Coalition and the host of the syndicated, evangelical radio program called *Focus on the Family*, is a layman who has become extremely and overtly political both on his radio program, and in other ways. Dobson recently endorsed a candidate for the office of Governor of Kansas at a rally held in Wichita. *The New York Times* reports:

> Between prayers and patriotic music, Mr. Dobson stood before a giant American flag and hailed Mr. Miller as a "man of courage, a man of conviction and a man of faith." He criticized Governor Graves, calling him "not pro-life, not pro-family and not conservative."[8]

Dobson not only used his evangelical credentials to endorse in the gubernatorial race in Kansas. He, along with fellow conservative Christians Pat Robertson and Jerry Falwell, also supported Alabama governor Fob James, Jr. in his primary race for re-election.[9] James earned their support through his outspoken advocacy of a return to prayer in schools and his defense of the display of religious symbols, such as the Ten Commandments, in public places such as court houses in Alabama. Following that election, in which Ralph Reed, formerly the Executive Director of the Christian Coalition, served as James' chief strategist, the power of the Religious Right in Southern politics was apparent. Alabama State Attorney General, Bill Pryor, stated, "Anyone who didn't think before that religious conservatives were a big part of the electorate here and the backbone of the Republican Party simply didn't understand Alabama."[10]

Dobson and Kennedy have also joined forces to create the Alliance Defense Fund, a legal group intended to counter-act the American Civil Liberties Union. The purpose of the group, according to its fundraising literature, is to "stop the homosexual agenda and protect traditional values."[11] To leave no doubt as to what "traditional values" might mean, Alan Sears, the group's President and General Counsel, says, "Over the years we hope to erect a wall of precedent that can't easily be breached by those who oppose Christian values."[12]

This phrase by Sears may sound innocent, even laudatory, but there is much in that phrase that causes concern insofar as the separation of church and state is concerned. First, who determines what those Christians values are that the Alliance Defense Fund presumes to be upholding? As this book has clearly indicated, there is no consensus within the Christian community on that question. Second, what do we do with the long-standing role of the First Amendment to the U.S. Constitution that protects the rights of religious minorities from the power of the majority group that may seek to impose its values upon the rest of society? Third, this is exactly what another leading evangelical, Carl F.H. Henry warned against when he said, "The church is not to use the mechanisms of government to legally impose upon society at large her theological commitments."[13]

FROM PULPIT TO POLITICS
The Religious Right and U.S. Foreign Policy

No doubt in reaction to the efforts of persons such as these, people express some reservation about having a member of the clergy in elective office. It may be that some voters think that by supporting such persons they are, in effect, advancing that conservative social agenda. The simple truth is, that agenda has already become the centerpiece of much of America's foreign and domestic policy. For instance, the United States has not paid its dues to The United Nations, largely because Jesse Helms, another conservative Christian and Chairman of the Senate Foreign Relations Committee, objects to the UN funding programs that teach birth control practices in Third World nations. Thus, the Pro-Life position is at the heart of that discussion, even though birth control and population planning are urgent issues for a global population that is about to exceed our ability to provide clean water, decent housing, and food for the people who presently occupy this planet.

FROM PULPIT TO POLITICS

It was reported in the June 17, 1998 issue of *The Cleveland Plain Dealer* that the nomination of James Hormel to be United States Ambassador to Luxembourg has been held up by Senate Majority Leader Trent Lott, largely because the nominee is a homosexual and is a supporter of gay causes. The article states:

> Trent Lott, the Mississippi Republican who controls the Senate agenda and opposes the Hormel nomination...said the Bible considers homosexuality a sin. David Smith, spokesman of the Human Rights Campaign, the nation's largest gay political group, said theologians may interpret the Bible differently but religious disagreement should never justify discriminatory public policy.[14]

It seems apparent that church and state are not nearly as separate as some in America might think or wish. The Religious Right has already become a major force in shaping American foreign and domestic policy, both through lobbying efforts and through direct support of candidates seeking political office. The challenge that confronts America at this point in time is to find ways to bring balance to the discussions and policy decisions that are already underway.

The nomination of James C. Hormel was eventually killed by the Senate Republican leadership by simply refusing to bring the nomination to a vote. The October 19 *New York Times* reports that Hormel would have been confirmed by the full Senate, so those who opposed him because he is openly gay found a way to prevent him from being confirmed as America's first openly gay ambassador.[15]

The Election of John F. Kennedy

The irony about the close bond between church and state within the white evangelical church community today is that this is essentially the same evangelical group that voiced strong opposition to the presidential aspirations of John F. Kennedy in 1960 on *precisely the same grounds*. As the first Roman Catholic since Al Smith, in 1928, to win the presidential nomination of a major political party, there was strong opposition to Kennedy's candidacy precisely on the grounds of separation of church and state. Charles Stewart, writing a chapter on "Separation of Church and State" in *Preaching in American History* by DeWitte Holland, notes that many sermons were preached in 1960 warning that the election of Kennedy would open the doors of the White House to the direct influence of the Pope in Rome. The fear was that Kennedy's election would result in the elevation of one religious tradition above all the others. "This could mean an end to religious liberty and the separation of church and state."[16] He quotes from one anti-Kennedy/anti-Catholic sermon preached in May, 1960, even before Kennedy received the Democratic Party nomination. It says in part:

> We call upon all Americans, let us pre-
> serve our Christian heritage for our won-
> derful children and their children. We
> must not turn our families over to Ca-
> tholicism by electing a Roman Catholic
> as President or Vice-President. NOW IS
> THE TIME TO STOP ROME'S
> MARCH INTO THE WHITE HOUSE.
> SPEAK UP...SPREAD THE

FROM PULPIT TO POLITICS

TRUTH...SAVE AMERICA...VOTE
AGAINST A ROMAN CATHOLIC FOR
PRESIDENT.[17]

Another sermon preached that same month declared, "If
you have a Roman Catholic President – he'll be backed
by nearly one hundred Roman Catholic members of the
House and a good number of Romans in the Senate."[18] It
is precisely that political influence that Southern Baptists now enjoy, without a whimper from within their
ranks about crossing the line that divides church and
state.

On September 12, 1960, Kennedy addressed those
concerns in a speech before the Houston (Texas) Ministerial Alliance. His comments on that occasion shed
considerable light on the relationship between church
and state in 1998. First he said:

> I believe in an America where the sepa-
> ration of church and state is absolute.
> Where no Catholic prelate would tell the
> President (should he be Catholic) how to
> act, and no Protestant minister would tell
> his parishioners for whom to vote –
> where no church or church school is

granted any public funds or political pref-
erence – and where no man is denied
public office merely because his religion
differs from the President who might ap-
point him or the people who might elect
him.[19]

The most famous lines in that speech came when Kennedy said:

I am not the Catholic candidate for President. I am the Democratic Party's candidate for President who happens also to be
a Catholic. I do not speak for my church
on public matters – and the church does
not speak for me...Whatever issues may
come before me as President – on birth
control, divorce, censorship, gambling or
any other subject – I will make my decision in accordance with what my conscience tells me to be the national interest, and without regard to outside religious pressures or dictates.[20]

The very same Protestant groups that spoke so vehemently against Kennedy's election have, in many instances, fallen far short of the separation of church and
state that Kennedy envisioned in this speech. John F.
Kennedy pledged, in 1960, to vote and consider public

FROM PULPIT TO POLITICS

policy based upon national interests and not narrow sectarian considerations. Active members of religious communities, lay and clergy, must make a similar pledge as they seek to serve in political office in the 1990s and beyond.

Kennedy was not the only President in recent memory that brought a strong religious affiliation into the White House. Jimmy Carter, also a Southern Baptist, continued to teach Sunday school when he visited his hometown of Plains, Georgia. In fact, his declaration in 1976 that he was "a born again Christian", may have opened the door to the kind of overt identification with a religious tradition that is so commonplace among evangelical groups in 1998. President Bill Clinton has made church attendance, with a Bible held prominently in his hand, a part of his political persona. Yet, neither Carter nor Clinton caused any expression of concern among these white, conservative Christians insofar as the undue influence of religion on public policy is concerned.

FROM PULPIT TO POLITICS

While evangelical Christians like the Christian Coalition and the Southern Baptist Convention may be the dominant group that bridges the once great divide between church and state in the white community, they were not the only Christians to enter the political waters in recent years. Two white members of the clergy join the seven black members, mentioned in Chapter Two, as members of the U.S. House of Representatives. Robert Edger, a Presbyterian minister and a six-term Congressman from Pennsylvania, was a member of the House Committee on Assassinations that investigated the deaths of President Kennedy and Martin Luther King, Jr. Father Robert Drinan, a Jesuit priest from Massachusetts, gained considerable fame while serving on the House Judiciary Committee during 1973 that considered impeachment proceedings against president Richard Nixon for his role in the so-called Watergate incident.

Still, even in 1998, with the great influence of the religious right, the white clergy in America does not play the same leadership role in the political arena as his/her black counter-part. There have been individual white clergy who have taken a stand on controversial political issues. One thinks immediately of William Sloane Coffin and his continual warnings against the construction and uses of nuclear weapons.[21] Philip and Daniel Berrigan, two brothers who were also Catholic priests, were outspoken critics of the war in Vietnam, and Daniel was actually arrested for trespassing on a nuclear weapons production facility.[22] Several white preachers and theologians, Reinhold Neibuhr and Walter Rauschenbusch among them, were frequent critics of American social policies that neglected the needs of America's poorest urban residents.[23] Even these two come in for special attention by James Cone who observes that few, if any, white theologians or preachers were outspoken on the issue of racism prior to the 1960s.[24] There may have been a scattered number of white preachers and denominational leaders who have issued statements and resolutions that touched upon one or another of the major social or political issues then confronting American society. The National Council of Churches and other state and local ecumenical groups have certainly functioned in this way. However, on the whole, the white clergy has not sought, or perhaps has not been able, to exercise much influence in the political life of this nation.

Clergy Leadership as a Matter of Necessity

Why have so few white clergy been active in the political arena throughout American history? Why have few white clergy from more moderate theological and doctrinal positions come forward to challenge the views and pronouncements of the Religious Right? Is this reluctance because these white clergy have felt restrained by the issue of separation of church and state? I submit this is not the principle reason for the absence of white clergy, either from elective office or from active involvement in political discussions. Instead, I would remind the reader of the historical circumstances that resulted in the necessity of the black preacher emerging as a political leader, circumstances that did not apply for the white preacher. From the founding of the nation to the present, there has never been a leadership shortage in the other professions, such as law or business, which usually feed people into political office, as there clearly was in the black community.

The words of Martin Delany in Chapter Three must be recalled. He acknowledges that the black preacher's influence and leadership outside of the church was in direct relationship to the fact that "colored men of other professions were in short supply.[25] Delany also observed that, "As among our people generally in 1849, the church is the alpha and omega of all things."[26] Neither of these factors that contributed to the influence of the black preacher was ever the case in the white community. The white clergy was never the sole source of leadership in that community, and the church was never preeminent above all other institutions for the white community in America.

Peter Dobkin Hall, in his book, *The Organization of American Culture, 1700-1900*, indicates that as far back as the colonial era the power and influence of the white clergy was being challenged by merchants, land owners, and lawyers. Hall states that in the seventeenth century "ministers were the only members of a learned profession to constitute a significant group in New England."[27] Things apparently changed in the eighteenth century, causing Hall to note that:

> By the early decades of the eighteenth century, clerical authority and the status of clergymen in their communities could only be maintained by actions that made clergymen dependent either on the legislature....or on powerful factions of the congregations, which were usually mercantile....Where once clergymen, as the only highly educated translocal group, had led the colonists, forming their opinions and serving as advisors and sometimes as masters of the magistrates, by the mid-eighteenth century they were struggling for survival...[28]

Even before the War of Independence, leadership and authority in white society had shifted away from the clergy to other professions.

FROM PULPIT TO POLITICS

Hall's comment that the clergy were dependent upon "powerful factions within the congregations", suggests that from the eighteenth century onward white clergy were often not even in charge of the affairs of their own congregations. This point is made even more explicitly, by Charles S. Sydnor in his book, *American Revolutionaries in the Making*. Rather than looking to the clergy, most matters in local parishes in colonial and post-Revolutionary America were entrusted to the twelve-member group in the Anglican or Episcopal Church called vestrymen. Sydnor observes:

> Construction of churches, the maintenance of ecclesiastical property, the supervision of spiritual affairs, the employment of ministers, the processioning of land according to the ancient custom for maintaining property boundaries, and the fixing of tithes to support the work of the parishes were the responsibility of vestries...[29]

In order to become a member of the vestry, Sydnor observes, one had to be a member of the landed gentry.

Frequently, such men were in control of both the secular and religious institutions of their community. He writes:

> Throughout the colonies a large share of the justices and higher political offices were vestrymen....Vestry, militia, and court were separate organizations; but the separation of ecclesiastical, military, and civil functions could not constitute a system of checks and balances so long as one man could hold office concurrently in all three organizations and often did.[30]

As a result, the white preacher never had to step forward, and might not have been allowed to step forward, to play the role of political leader, because there have always been others in the white community who were available to play that role.

Anxiety about State-Sanctioned Churches

Added to this factor of non-necessity, was another lingering concern that many whites in America may have had from the colonial era forward. This concern, vaguely articulated, but pervasive and long-lasting, was over the repression that colonists attached to the existence of a state-sanctioned church, such as many of them experienced or recalled, either in Europe or in colonial America. The concern involved such things as being required to pay a tax to support the state sanctioned church, even if you were not a member of that religious group. It also included such concerns as the use of coercion to prevent a person from practicing the religion of their choice, or to force them to swear allegiance to that state sanctioned practice.

Many groups, including Jews, Catholics, Mormons, Quakers, and others have known this anxiety. It was clearly to protect the rights of these religious minorities, and those in America who decided to engage in no religious practices at all, that the First Amendment to the U.S. Constitution was included. It is in light of this history that the comments by Alan Sears of the Alliance Defense Fund, pledging to protect "Christian values", cause such anxiety in an American society that reflects even more religious diversity today than it did in 1791

FROM PULPIT TO POLITICS

when the First Amendment was ratified and added to the
U.S. Constitution.

It seems apparent at this point in American history,
however, that the establishment of a state church is neither the topic of discussion or the object of any particular concern among any segment of American society.
Today, the concern over the separation of church and
state is much more a matter of whether clergy, or faith-
based organizations, will attempt to impose some sectarian agenda upon public policy. The concern takes two
distinct forms. First, such groups as The Christian Coalition and The Family Research Center have already
talked about seeking to have the U.S. Constitution
amended to ban abortion funding and certain abortion
procedures, and to guarantee a restoration of prayer in
schools. Second, these same groups have begun target-
ing either the election or defeat of certain lawmakers, as
with the gubernatorial races this year in Alabama and
Kansas.[31] Either way, the Religious Right has entered

the political fray undeterred by philosophical arguments about the separation of church and state.

The Religious Right and the Republican Party

The stage has long since been set for religious leaders who favor this social agenda to be sought out by the most influential politicians in the nation who are looking for votes and support. The annual meeting of The Christian Coalition was held in Washington, D.C. on September 18, 1998. Richard Berke writing for *The New York Times*, notes that "several presidential hopefuls seized the opportunity to emphasize their religious and conservative credentials to core Republicans who are crucial in the party's primaries."[32] Berke mentions that among the high profile political leaders who addressed The Christian Coalition at its opening plenary session were Senate Majority Leader Trent Lott, House Speaker Newt Gingrich, House Majority Leader Dick Armey, and House Majority Whip Tom Delay. They were all joined by The Rev. Pat Robertson, founder of The Christian

192

Coalition, and himself a two-time former Presidential hopeful in the Republican Party.

If there is a clear and present risk to the separation of church and state, it is through this alliance of religious and political conservative forces allied not around "liberty and justice for all", but around a punitive social contract that could be damaging to the rights and freedoms of African Americans, women, those living in poverty and on welfare, and religious minorities.

Moderate White Clergy Must Step Forward

I do not condemn the religious right and their political allies, because they are, in their own way, seeking to live up to the words of Robert McAfee Brown and turn "politics into a means of grace."[33] I simply refuse to allow their social agenda to stand, unchallenged, as the essence of what constitutes the center of Christian social concern. I sought political office because I saw that as an opportunity to stand against what I see as a dangerous alliance between two formidable, conservative forces. I

193

urge other committed Christians, clergy and lay, with an
agenda centered around justice for all people, to also
seek public office.

If they are not successful in their pursuit of elective
office, they need to find other ways to advance the issues
and causes that concern them. There is too much at stake
to just sit on the sideline while the existing religious and
political alliance between the Republican Party and the
Religious Right pursue their agenda. There is no question that Ralph Reed is right when he observes that
"People of faith now play a major role in policy and political elections."[34] My concern is that the people of faith
who are presently engaged in the political process, and
who are exerting tremendous influence on domestic and
foreign policy, do not reflect the interests and concerns
of many segments of American society.

The voices of white clergy who do not see themselves being represented by Jerry Falwell, Pat Robertson
and D. James Kennedy must be heard. They cannot allow a mis-interpretation of the principle of separation of

church and state keep them from being actively involved
in the policy discussions that are now underway. The
Religious Right is already on the field. Who from the
ranks of the white Christian community in America will
step forward to contend with them?

Many black preachers are attempting to offer alternative visions of how the Christian faith should interface
with public policy. That is the legacy of Martin Luther
King, Jr., and those who carry on in his spirit. Now as
then, however, the problem is the appalling silence of so
many good people. In 1963, King wrote, *"The Letter
From the Birmingham Jail"*, in response to comments
from eight white clergy in that segregated, Southern city
who condemned him for his presence in Birmingham,
and for his sharp attacks on that city's social structure.
King responded by saying:

> The contemporary church is often a weak,
> ineffectual voice with an uncertain sound.
> It is so often the arch-supporter of the
> status quo. Far from being disturbed by
> the presence of the church, the power
> structure of the average community is

consoled by the church's silent and often
vocal sanction of things as they are....I
hope the church as a whole will meet the
challenge of this decisive hour.[35]

Thirty-five years have passed since King wrote those
words to white clergy in Birmingham, and the need for
their response is just as urgent today. The Religious
Right has staked out its agenda. The time is now for "the
whole church to meet the challenge of this decisive
hour." Among the ways by which they can respond, is to
make the move *From Pulpit to Politics*.

Notes: Chapter Five

[1]Laurie Goodstein. "Look Who's Leading the Country", The New York Times 14 June 1998: A4.
[2]Allison Mitchell. "Gay Behavior Is Described As A Sin By Lott", The New York Times 16 June 1998: A24.
[3]Jill Lawrence. "In Iowa, Republicans Come Out of the Values Closet", USA Today 15 June 1998: A14.
[4]Lawrence A14.
[5]Lawrence A14.
[6]Lawrence A14.

FROM PULPIT TO POLITICS

[7]Kevin Sack. "Ralph Reed Aims to Broaden Social Conservatives' Appeal", The New York Times@aol.com: 1.

[8]Dirk Johnson. "A Race for the Souls of the Suburbs", The New York Times 1 July 1998: A12.

[9]"Right Strikes a Blow in the Heart of Dixie", The New York Times 2 July 1998: A15

[10]The New York Times A15.

[11]"The ACLU Finally Meets Its Match", Newsletter of the Alliance Defense Fund PO Box 54370, Phoenix, AZ.

[12]Newsletter of the Alliance Defense Fund 2.

[13]Carl F.H. Henry. Christian Countermoves in a Decadent Culture (Portland, OR: Multanomah Press, 1986) 118.

[14]"Vote Requested on Gay Nominee", The Cleveland Plain Dealer 17 June 1998: 15A.

[15]Philip Shenon. "Gay Philanthropist's Nomination to Become Ambassador to Luxembourg Dies in the Senate", The New York Times, 19 October 1998: A1.

[16]Dewitte Holland. Preaching in American History. (Nashville, TN: Abingdon Press, 1969).

[17]Holland 158.

[18]Holland 158.

[19]John F. Kennedy. "Address of Senator John F. Kennedy to the Greater Houston Ministerial Association", Rice Hotel, Houston, Texas, 12 Sept. 1960.

[20]Kennedy 12 Sept. 1960.

FROM PULPIT TO POLITICS

[21]Jane Rockman, ed. Peace in Search of Makers. (Valley Forge. PA: Judson Press, 1979) 7-11.

[22]Jim Wallis and Joyce Hollyday. Cloud of Witnesses. (Maryknoll, NY: Orbis Books, 1991) 221- 227.

[23]Cf. Reinhold Niebuhr. Moral Man and Immoral Society. (New York: Scribners, 1932) and Frank Hoadley and Benjamin Browne. Baptists Who Dared. (Valley Forge, PA: Judson Press,1980) 79-82.

[24]James Cone. A Black Theology of Liberation. (Philadelphia: Lippincott, 1970) 30-31.

[25]Benjamin Quarles. Black Abolitionists. (New York: Da Capo Press, 1969) 69.

[26]Quarles 69.

[27]Peter Dobkin Hall. The Organization of American Culture. (New York: New York University Press, 1984) 25.

[28]Hall 30.

[29]Charles Sydnor. American Revolutionaries in the Making. (New York: Free Press, 1952) 83.

[30]Syndor 85.

[31]Johnson A12.

[32]Richard Berke. "To Christians, G.O.P. Urges Punishment and Prayer", The New York Times 19 Sept. 1998: A9

[33]Robert McAfee Brown, "Confessions of a Political Neophyte", Christianity and Crisis, Volume XII, No 24 19 Jan. 1953: 186.

FROM PULPIT TO POLITICS

[34]Albert R. Hunt, "The Religious Right Is About Politics, Not Faith", The Wall Street Journal 20 Aug. 1998: A15.

[35]Martin Luther King, Jr. Why We Can't Wait. (New York: Signet Books, 1963) 91-92.

FROM PULPIT TO POLITICS

EPILOGUE: It Is Our Duty

Two of the most renowned black preachers of the 20th century, Samuel D. Proctor and Gardner C. Taylor, collaborated on a book entitled, *We Have This Ministry*.[1] Both of them have been directly involved in politics and government service while continuing their involvement with preaching and/or pastoral ministry. Proctor served in the Kennedy Administration as Director of the Peace Corps in Nigeria, and in the Johnson Administration as Director of the Office of Economic Opportunity. Taylor served on the New York City Board of Education, and contemplated a run for a seat in the U.S. Congress in the 1960s. In this book, they both reflect upon the relationship between the preacher and politics.

The comments of these two men on the issue of preachers and politics are especially important to me, because they have played such a decisive role in my own career. I served as an assistant to Samuel Proctor from 1972-1976 at Abyssinian Baptist Church in New York City. Much of what I know about pastoral leadership and social responsibility I learned by watching and listening to him. I studied preaching with Gardner Taylor at Union Theological Seminary in the 1970s. I have sat under his preaching on scores of occasions, and have sought his advice and insight on every major career decision in my twenty-two years in the ministry. When these two men speak about the role of the black preacher in politics I want to listen.

Proctor identifies the areas in American society where the black preacher needs to be actively engaged. He challenges preachers to work for economic opportunity, to advocate for the poor and the sick, to use all available means to shape public opinion and public policy, to impact the quality of public education, and to be a prophetic voice from the pulpit on issues of justice and compassion.[2] He does not specifically challenge preachers to run for political office in an attempt to address and empower his list of concerns. However, he suggests that today's preachers must work to advance the great social crusades of the past that have made this nation more just and humane. He lists such societal advances as women's suffrage, the abolition of slavery, the creation of Medicare, Medicaid and Social Security, all of which were politically derived advances.[3] Whether through holding office, or working in some other way to advance a political agenda, it seems apparent that Proctor sees a close link between the pulpit and politics. It is a link that he himself embodied for nearly a decade of his own life.

Gardner Taylor once considered running for Congress. While he did not pursue that office, he did serve on the Board of Education in New York City, and does concede that for many years he enjoyed "political prominence" in that city.[4] In terms of the appropriateness of the black preacher running for office, Taylor offers the following comment:

> I have often been asked whether a pastor should ever consider running for political office. I say yes, when there are no other credible candidates. A pastor who is elected to public office can exert a real influence for good.[5]

FROM PULPIT TO POLITICS

As one who served in elective office, Taylor offers several warnings of what can happen to a preacher's credibility and pastoral focus if he or she were to become active in politics. People may wonder if the things a preacher says are colored more by the scriptures or political expediency. "The moment you become identified too closely with any segment of the political undertaking, you lose a certain moral ground and objectivity."[6]

Having said that, Taylor, like Proctor, points to the litany of crises in America to which the preacher must respond. They include corporate down-sizing and the loss of jobs in urban areas, the increased incidences of AIDS, the continuing problem of drug abuse, the sanctity of human life *outside* as well as inside the womb, and the persistent problem of racism. By his own personal example, Taylor acknowledges that politically involved preachers can work to accomplish what has repeatedly been referenced from Robert McAfee Brown and Carl F.H. Henry. When Christians are involved in politics, it can become "a means of grace."[7] And when

FROM PULPIT TO POLITICS

Christians are involved in politics, that arena becomes an environment in which justice can be preserved and disorder can be restrained.[8]

I have long believed that one of the most compelling images of the role of the preacher is found in Isaiah 21 and Ezekiel 33, which talk about "the watchman." The preacher is one whose job it is to remain observant to what is happening in the community, to what dangers can be seen on the horizon, and to loudly sound the warning. The passage in Isaiah is especially poignant, because it finds the community turning to the watchman for some word of assurance or direction. *"Watchman, what of the night?"*

Preachers across this nation, and black preachers in particular, must serve as watchmen for American society. There are four roles out of which they can respond to whatever dangers they see approaching; according to Peter Paris; priestly, prophetic, political and nationalistic. This book is designed to encourage preachers, and other committed people of faith, to view the political arena as a legitimate and appropriate way of responding to the dangers that greatly threaten our society and our planet.

Not all preachers will choose to accept this challenge to aggressively engage the political process. They may prefer to remain within the priestly mode, or to challenge the status quo from the posture of prophetic preaching. It is my hope that none will become so frustrated with the possibility of a truly multi-cultural and inter-racial society that they opt for a nationalist approach. In the end, however, each person must find his or her own way. But each person must find some way to answer the call from Isaiah 21:11, *"Watchman, what of the night?"* Insofar as this book is concerned, however, one of the best ways to respond to the dangers and dilemmas so powerfully detailed by Proctor and Taylor is by making the move *From Pulpit to Politics!*

Notes: Epilogue

[1]Samuel D. Proctor and Gardner C. Taylor. We Have This Ministry. (Valley Forge, PA: Judson Press, 1996).
[2]Proctor 111-126.
[3]Proctor 116.
[4]Proctor 131.
[5]Proctor 129.
[6]Proctor 129.
[7]Robert McAfee Brown. "Confessions of a Political Neophyte", Christianity and Crisis, Volume XII No. 24 19 Jan. 1953: 186.
[8]Carl F. H. Henry. Christian Countermoves in a Decadent Culture. (Portland, OR: Multanomah Press, 1986): 118.

FROM PULPIT TO POLITICS

Bibliography

"The ACLU Finally Meets Its Match", <u>Newsletter of the Alliance Defense Fund</u> PO Box 54370, Phoenix, AZ.

Allen, Mike. "Cardinal Sees Marriage Harm in Partners Bill", <u>The New York Times</u> 25 May 1998, 1A.

Bellah, Robert N. <u>The Broken Covenant</u>. New York: Seabury Press, 1975.

Bennett, John C. <u>Christians and the State</u>. New York: Scribners, 1958.

Berke, Richard. "To Christians, G.O.P. Urges Punishment and Prayer", <u>The New York Times</u> 19 Sept. 1998: A9

Briggs, David. "Civil-Society Panel Addresses Moral Decline and Malaise", <u>The Cleveland Plain Dealer</u>, 28 May 1998: 7A.

Briggs, David. "U.S. Catholics Urged to Take Abortion Issue to Ballot Box", <u>The Cleveland Plain Dealer</u>, 29 Oct. 1998: 1A.

Brotz, Howard, ed. <u>Negro Social and Political Thought</u>. New York: Basic Books, 1966.

Brown, Robert McAfee. "Confessions of a Political Neophyte", <u>Christianity and Crisis, Volume XII No. 24</u> (19 Jan. 1953).

Carrelli, Richard. "Alabama's Appeal on Prayer Rejected", <u>The Cleveland Plain Dealer</u> 23 June, 1998: 1A.

FROM PULPIT TO POLITICS

Carter, Stephen L. <u>The Culture of Disbelief</u>. New York: Anchor Books, 1994.

Carter, Stephen L. <u>The Dissent of the Governed: A Meditation On Law, Religion and Loyalty</u>. Cambridge, MA: Harvard, 1998.

Cone, James. <u>A Black Theology of Liberation</u>. Philadelphia: Lippincott, 1970.

Drake, St. Clair and Horace Clayton. <u>Black Metropolis: A Study of Negro Life in a Northern City</u>. University of Chicago Press, 1945.

Du Bois, W.E.B. <u>The Souls of Black Folk</u>. Greenwhich, CN: Fawcett Books.

Fant, Clyde Jr. and William Pinson, Jr. <u>20 Centuries of Great Preaching, Volume 12</u> Waco, TX: Word Books, 1971.

Farclough, Adam. <u>To Redeem the Soul of America</u>. Athens: University of Georgia, 1987.

Fineman, Howard. "The Gospel of St. John", <u>Newsweek</u>, 1 June 1998.

Fitts, Leon. <u>Lott Carey: First Black Missionary to Africa</u>. Valley Forge, PA: Judson Press, 1978.

Foner, Eric. <u>A Short History of Reconstruction</u>. New York: Norton, 1989.

Gedicks, Frederick M.. "The Religious, the Secular and the Anti-thetical", <u>Capital U. Law Review 20</u>, (1991).

Gomes, Peter. <u>The Good Book</u>. New York: Avon Books, 1996.

Goodstein, Laurie. "Look Who's Leading the Country", The New York Times 14 June 1998: A4.

Goodstein, Laurie. "Town's Logo Becomes a Religious Battleground", The New York Times. 23 June 1998: 1A

Hall, Peter Dobkin. The Organization of American Culture. New York: New York University Press, 1984.

Hallett, Joe. "Candidates Seek Black Ministers' Support", The Cleveland Plain Dealer 29 April 1998: 1A.

Hallett, Joe. "Storming the Churches", The Cleveland Plain Dealer, 3 May 1998: 1A.

Hallett, Joe. "11th District Race Was Too Clean to See", The Cleveland Plain Dealer, 8 May, 1998: 11B.

Hamilton, Charles V. The Black Preacher in America. New York: Morrow, 1972.

Henry, Carl F.H.. Christian Countermoves in a Decadent Culture. Portland, OR: Multnomah Press, 1986.

Holland, Dewitte, ed. Sermons in American History. Nashville: Abingdon Press, 1971.

Holland, Dewitte. Preaching in American History. Nashville, TN: Abingdon Press,1969.

Hughes, Langston. "Let America Be America Again", Hope and History by Vincent Harding. Maryknoll, NY: Orbis Books, 1990.

Hunt, Albert R. "The Religious Right Is About Politics, Not Faith", The Wall Street Journal, 20 Aug. 1998, A15.

"Jefferson Davis", Webster's American Biographies.
Springfield, MA: G. and C. Merriam Co., 1974.

Johnson, Dirk. "A Race for the Souls of the Suburbs",
The New York Times 1 July 1998: A12.

Johnson, James Weldon. God's Trombones. New York:
Viking Press, 1969.

Johnson, Sherman E. "Matthew", The Interpreter's Bible
Volume 7, Nashville, TN: Abingdon Press, 1958.

Kennedy, John F. "Address of Senator John F. Kennedy
to the Greater Houston Ministerial Association",
Rice Hotel, Houston, Texas, 12 Sept. 1960.

Kennedy, John W. "Wild Card Election", Christianity
Today, 26 Oct., 1998: 82.

King, Martin Luther, Jr. Why We Can't Wait. New
York: Signet Books, 1963.

Koch, Adriene and William Rede. The Life and Selected
Writings of Thomas Jefferson. New York: The Modern Library, 1944.

Lawrence, Jill. "In Iowa, Republicans Come Out of the
Values Closet", USA Today 15 June 1998: A14.

Litwack, Leon. Black Leaders of the Nineteenth Century. Urbana: University of Illinois Press, 1991.

Litwack, Leon. North of Slavery: The Negro in the Free
States 1790-1860. University of Chicago Press,
1961.

Maddox, Robert L. Separation of Church and State. New
York: Crossroads, 1987.

McMickle, Marvin A. "A Million Men Minus One", The
Cleveland Plain Dealer, 13 Oct. 1995: editorial page.

Miller, Kelly. Out of the House of Bondage. New York: Schocken Books, 1971.

Mitchell, Allision. "Gay Behavior Is Described As A Sin By Lott", The New York Times 16 June 1998: A24.

Morris, Aldon E. Origins of the Civil Rights Movement. New York: The Free Press, 1984.

Moses, William Jeremiah. The Golden Age of Black Nationalism. New York: Oxford, 1978.

Neuhaus, Richard. The Naked Public Square: Religion and Democracy in America. Grand Rapids, MI: Eerdman, 1984.

Cf. Niebuhr, Reinhold. Moral Man and Immoral Society. New York: Scribners, 1932 and Hoadley, Frank and Benjamin Browne. Baptists Who Dared. Valley Forge, PA: Judson Press,1980.

Novak, Michael. "Answering the Big Questions", The Cleveland Plain Dealer 2 June 1998: 9B.

Ofari, Earl. Let Your Motto Be Resistance. Boston: Beacon Press, 1972.

Paris, Peter. Black Religious Leaders. Louisville, KY: Westminster/John Knox Press, 1991.

Proctor, Samuel D. and Gardner C. Taylor. We Have This Ministry. Valley Forge, PA: Judson Press, 1996.

Quarles, Benjamin. Black Abolitionists. New York: Da Capo Press, 1969.

Quarles, Benjamin. The Negro and the Civil War. New York: Da Capo Press, 1989.

Reported to me in a conversation with Dr. Fred Finks, President of Ashland Theological Seminary, Ashland, OH.

"Right Strikes a Blow in the Heart of Dixie", The New York Times 2 July 1998: A15.

Rockman, Jane, ed. Peace in Search of Makers. Valley Forge. PA: Judson Press, 1979.

Rollenhagen, Mark. "Prosecutors Outline Corruption Case", The Cleveland Plain Dealer, 27 Oct., 1998: 1B.

Sack, Kevin. "Atlanta Rally Unburdened by Ills of Harlem's", The New York Times@aol.com,: 8 Sept. 1998: 1.

Sack, Kevin. "Ralph Reed Aims to Broaden Social Conservatives' Appeal", The New York Times@aol.com: 1.

Shenon, Philip. "Gay Philanthropist's Nomination to Become Ambassador to Luxembourg Dies in the Senate", The New York Times, 19 Oct., 1998: 1A.

Sherry, Paul H. The Riverside Preachers. New York: Pilgrim Press, 1978.

Stokes, Carl B. Promises of Power: Then and Now. Cleveland: Friends of Carl B. Stokes, 1989.

Syndor, Charles. American Revolutionaries in the Making. New York: Free Press, 1952.

Tate, Katherine. From Protest to Politics. Cambridge, MA: Harvard, 1993.

Thomas, Gary. "The Return of the Jewish Church", Christianity Today, 7 Sept. 1998.

Thomas, John L. Slavery Attacked: The Abolitionist Crusade. Englewood Cliffs, NJ: Prentice Hall, 1965.

Tinsley, Jessie. "Saving the Soul of the City", The Cleveland Plain Dealer Sunday Magazine, 30 Aug. 1998.

"Vote Requested on Gay Nominee", The Cleveland Plain Dealer 17 June 1998: 15A.

Wallis, Jim and Joyce Hollyday. Cloud of Witnesses. Maryknoll, NY: Orbis Books, 1991.

Washington, James M. Frustrated Fellowship: The Baptist Quest for Social Power. (Macon, GA: Mercer University Press, 1986.

Washington, James M. Testament of Hope. New York: Harper and Row, 1989.

Wilmore, Gayraud. Black Religion and Black Radicalism. Garden City, NJ: Anchor Books, 1972.

Woodson, Carter G. History of the Negro Church. Washington, D.C.: The Association Press, 1972.

Woorward, C. Vann. The Strange Career of Jim Crow. New York: Oxford, 1973.